# A Complete Guide to
# SERMON DELIVERY

*vocal production*

*facial expression*

*eye contact*

*posture*

*articulation*

*gestures*

# AL FASOL

BROADMAN
& HOLMAN
PUBLISHERS

Nashville, Tennessee

© 1996 by Al Fasol
All rights reserved
Printed in the United States of America

Published by:
Broadman & Holman Publishers
Nashville, Tennessee

Design:
Steven Boyd

4212-40
0-8054-1240-9

Acquistions and Development Editor: John Landers

Dewey Decimal Classification: 251.03
Subject Heading: PREACHING
Library of Congress Card Catalog Number: 95-50580

**Library of Congress Cataloging-in-Publication Data**
Fasol, Al.
  A complete guide to sermon delivery / Al Fasol.
    p.  cm.
  ISBN 0-8054-1240-9 (pbk.)
  1.Preaching.  2.Public speaking—Religious aspects—Christianity.
I. Title.
  BV4211.2.F41996
  251'.03—dc20
  95-50580
  CIP

01 02 03 04 05 06 01 00 99 98 97 96

*To:*
*Zach, Mallory, and Mollie McMeans,*
*my triplet grandchildren*

# CONTENTS

# PREFACE

$P$reaching is a fascinating study that integrates a number of theological and communication disciplines. H. C. Brown, Jr., contended that "True homiletics involves . . . the correct use of Biblical content, hermeneutical principles, theological perspectives, psychological orientation, rhetorical rules, and oratorical principles."[1] This book focuses on oratorical principles; that is, the vocal/physical delivery of a sermon.

Sermon delivery should not be isolated as a homiletic discipline—even for analytical purposes. In fact, this book is based on the presupposition that sermon delivery derives its reason for existence from its relationship to sermon content. That relationship may be specified as one that *maximizes the message and minimizes the messenger.* Too often the opposite is true. But that fact simply affirms the need for this book. The preaching models for too many of us have been, "What I say is not so important as how I say it." To compound this unfortunate approach to preaching, the "how I say it" is usually either awful, mediocre, or dismissed as "the way preachers talk." To compound the misfortune, many congregations have come to expect a good sermon to be (1) pious speech that sounds religious, whether or not it is biblical, (2) a performance by the preacher, and (3) a presentation by one who speaks loudly and rapidly in a rough, gravelly voice.

Some people maintain that sermon delivery cannot be taught because it reflects the preacher's personality. This is partially true. Sermon delivery *is* an extension of the preacher's personality, but personalities can and should mature and grow. Improvement in sermon delivery is, of course, one key area in which the person who preaches must grow. Speech functions *can* be taught—even to preachers.

As a teacher of homiletics, I admit that I cannot teach motivation for preaching. Much of the success of preaching depends on the individual's inner drives. However, a study of sermon delivery can help improve communication. In fact, sermon delivery that is forceful, appealing, and clear is a blessing to any congregation. Yet excellence in delivery should spring from the minister's dedication to a divine call to preach. The success of preaching lies in an inner sense of dedication, not in the mastery of speech techniques. This book seeks to enhance the dedicated, God-called preacher's ability to communicate. We have already established the definite need for that enhancement.

I use the word *speaker* synonymously with the word *preacher* because this book is written for anyone in God's service who wishes to improve his or her ability to communicate. *Speaker* is used when application can be made beyond preaching. *Preacher* is used when application should be made primarily to the preacher.

I hope this book will immediately help the preacher improve sermon delivery. I do not want to produce another boring speech book. I look forward to responses from students, for they assuredly will relate to me how close my ambitions for this book have come to being achieved.

My appreciation is extended to my friends: to Dr. Jimmie L. Nelson, whose critical reading and pertinent suggestions were helpful; to Dr. Michael Graves, who shared responses from his students related to this book; and to Mrs. Laverne Smith, who typed the final draft. As always, responsibility for the product is mine.

▼

*The sermon itself is the main thing: its matter, its aim, and the spirit in which it is brought before the people, the sacred anointing upon the preacher, and the divine power applying the truth to the hearer—these are infinitely more important than any details of manner. Posture and action are comparatively small and inconsiderable matters, but still even the sandal in the statue of Minerva should be correctly carved, and in the service of God even the smallest things should be regarded with holy care.*

Charles Haddon Spurgeon
*Lectures to My Students*

▼

# Introduction

Sermon delivery is the servant of sermon content. This relationship must be understood and practiced if preaching is to be effective. What we preach is always more important than how we preach. Note carefully that the relationship between content and delivery is stated in the comparative degree: Content is more important than delivery. Delivery is important, but content is more important. This basic and specialized statement of a theology of proclamation is the foundation of this book. The purpose of this introduction is to present a basic theology of sermon delivery.

Our working definition of preaching is this: Preaching is a word from God applied to a contemporary congregation, communicated by a God-called person in a way that maximizes the message and minimizes the messenger.

Domenico Grasso concluded, "The object and content of the preaching of Jesus and the Apostles is the person of Christ."[1] "Unlike all other messages, the Christian message is identified with the Messenger, with the person of Christ."[2] According to Grasso, preaching should be identifiable with Christ.

Karl Barth felt that preaching should be the speaking of the Word of God. This speaking should involve the listener in the Word of God in a way that removes the barriers of time. In true biblical preaching, Barth contended, the listener should not think in terms of first century and twentieth century, but consider the central truth of the Word of God. Barth affirmed that biblical preaching dissolves the wall between the first-century word and twentieth-century man.[3] But what should preaching do? "What is transmitted and what one seeks to have accepted is a person. And the goal to be obtained is adherence to a person. . . . The real problem of preaching consists in discovering how to . . . establish between God and man a community of life, so that man will not think of or see himself except in the light of God."[4]

Schleiermacher taught that preaching should be an opportunity for the Word to rise forth from the spiritual union of the preacher with his listeners, and that preaching should give expression to the life in which preacher and congregation are thus joined.[5]

Perhaps Schleiermacher sounds a little "heady," and more than a little idealistic. Clyde Fant writes, "The passionate desire to insure that the pure Word of God is proclaimed to the congregation has resulted in an almost superstitious depersonalization of the act of preaching. As a matter of practical fact, the Word does not 'arise out of the Bible and proceed into the congregation.' It proceeds into the congregation on the words of a very subjective human being who has struggled to interpret those words which he has found in the Bible and which God graces with his presence as the Word."[6]

These excerpts are included to stimulate the preacher's thinking about how one preaches. Such evaluation will sharpen understanding of the relation between text, sermon, and sermon delivery. Nebulous thinking results in nebulous preaching, and nebulous preaching is never appropriate. Sermon content (what we preach) must be strong, clear, text-centered, and supported by effective delivery.

## Who Should Preach: A God-Called Person

Communication is a diverse discipline that is foundational to preaching. When we preach, all that we are as Christian persons is focused on communicating a message from God. Our childhood experiences, our conversion experience, our models in preaching and pastoring, our self-image, our perception of what preaching should be and what preaching should do, and our various academic and theological studies are but a few of the resources we call on as we prepare to preach. When we deliver the sermon, these resources are brought into tension with individuals who have their own varying perceptions of who they are, who and what the preacher is, what preaching should be, and what it should do. Our varying backgrounds will either assist the preacher in achieving desired responses from the congregation or, at times, hinder the preacher from achieving desired responses. They may even elicit an undesired response from the congregation.

Communication is a fascinating, complex process. Broadly defined, communication means "to pass along information by talking, writing, or gesturing." The process is not automatic. The steps to sermon delivery discussed in this book are designed to help Christian communicators bring their individual communication skills to maturity.

## How We Should Preach: Maximizing the Message and Minimizing the Messenger

Sermon delivery derives its importance from its relationship to sermon content. The goal of sermon delivery is to maximize the message and minimize the messenger. The messenger is a critically important part of the preaching process, but the messenger is never more important than the message. As sermon delivery derives its importance from its relationship to sermon content, so the messenger derives importance from the message to be delivered. The preacher, for instance, is not like a mail deliverer. The person who delivers the mail has a noble vocation, but once the mail is delivered the task is completed. The preacher's responsibilities continue beyond the mere delivery of the message.

The preacher may be compared to an ambassador who represents higher officials, nations, or kingdoms. The ambassador is entrusted to speak for another. The ambassador cultivates relationships with those being represented and also with those who receive this representative. These relationships help the ambassador know who is being represented and why. When the ambassador conveys a message, it is more likely to be communicated accurately and efficiently. Furthermore, those who receive the message need to know something about the messenger. The ambassador therefore must convince those receiving the message that the messenger is a person of expertise and integrity and possesses deep convictions about the message.

Why go through all this work? Why not just imitate some outstanding preacher? When God called you to preach, he saw something in you, some quality no one else has. He called you to be you, not someone else. To imitate someone else is tantamount to saying to God, "You used poor judgment in calling me, God. Since you obviously made a mistake, then I will help you correct it. Instead of being me, I will be someone else for you." God knew what he was doing when he called you. To give him less than the best you can be by imitating someone else is to insult God's judgment. Furthermore, persons who imitate other speakers almost always imitate their weaknesses rather than their strengths. (Even the best of preachers could stand improvement.) Persons who imitate them generally imitate their pitch patterns or some other distracting mannerism. Rather than insulting God and perpetuating some inappropriate delivery style, dedicate yourself to being the best communicator God can make of you.

What are the criteria for measuring effectiveness in delivery? Are these criteria always subjective? Will they be the same in all preaching situations? in all denominations? in all regions of the country or world? for all the various styles of preaching? The complexities are endless, but some guidelines are available. They will be discussed in the next chapters of this book.

One additional aspect of sermon delivery should be discussed here. Much of the communication of a sermon takes place before the first word is preached. The pastoral role produces varying relationships between pastor and congregation. If these relationships are positive, the congregation will receive the pastor as a person of credibility, as someone in whom they can believe. Creating this positive feeling is as critical in preaching as it is in any form of communication (as, for example, the analogy of the ambassador cited earlier).

Every congregation or audience needs to know that the preacher or speaker is (1) a person of competence, a person "who knows what he is talking about"; (2) a person of integrity, a person who can be trusted, not a manipulator or exploiter; and (3) a person of vitality, a preacher who communicates a deep sense of belief in all that is said. The messenger's credibility with the congregation is critical in preaching. When credibility is present the congregation is free to respond, to interact with the message as well as the messenger. Without it, the preacher faces a congregation that is fettered by a lack of confidence in the messenger and therefore the message. The apostle Paul faced a credibility problem in Corinth. He did not appeal to the Corinthians to defend his reputation so that he would be received, but so that his message would be received. Paul based his plea on an appeal to his integrity: "We are made manifest unto God; and I trust also are made manifest in your consciences" (2 Cor. 5:11b). "Manifest" means literally, "to be turned inside out." This was Paul's way of saying, "I have no ulterior or suspicious motives. What you see is a man devoted to God's service. What you get is what you see."

This introduction has sketched a theology of sermon delivery. The following chapters are devoted to the mechanics of sermon delivery that support content, seeking to maximize the message and minimize the messenger.

▼

# O N E

*You know these are the days of sore throats . . .
among preachers. Some have laid the predisposing
cause to coffee, and some to tobacco. . . . Now,
without professing to have studied physiology, or to
be skilled in the science of medicine, I beg leave,
with very humble pretensions, to give it as my
opinion that most cases . . . are brought on by care-
lessness . . . of public speakers themselves.*

Peter Cartwright
*An Autobiography*

▼

# Achieving Full Vocal Production

The preacher came to the time of application in the conclusion of his evangelistic sermon. His words were incisive, and they were a direct appeal to non-Christians in the congregation. He said, *"Do you know what you need? You need Jesus!"* The content of his application was strong and accurate. Unfortunately, few people could understand what he said. That was because the question, "Do you know what you need?" was preached in a gravelly, strained, extremely high-pitched voice. He literally gave the question all the vocal emphasis he could muster. He had no vocal range left for the next words of his sermon. Consequently, the answer to his question, "You need Jesus!" was vocalized in a rushed, hissing sound. This "dramatic whisper" had no distinguishable words. If we were to spell his sounds, "You need Jesus" came out something like this: "yeh knee sheeses." He presumed the congregation would figure out what he said. His most important words, "You need Jesus," were not understood. The only non-Christian in the congregation had no idea, contextually or otherwise, what these hissing sounds meant. The content was fine, but the delivery was a total failure. The use of full vocal production could have helped that preacher communicate his message clearly and strongly.

This preacher was only forty-three years old at the time that the sermon was preached, but he had been abusing his voice since his call to preach eighteen years before. In fact, he thought that he *had* to strain his voice in order to sound like a preacher. After all, almost every preacher he ever heard strained his voice, and some of them were great men of God. He presumed good preachers strained their voices and "dry" preachers did not. Following this stereotype guaranteed him a sore throat every Sunday, hoarseness on Monday, and permanent vocal damage by the time he was forty-six years old.

His misconceptions about preaching were brought about, at least in part, by the notion that *what* he preached was less important than *how* he preached. Unfortunately, this fallacy has persisted. Many otherwise able servants of God preach in a way that hinders their communication of the gospel and cripples their ability to speak. That man lost his voice just as he entered his prime as a preacher. It was a tragic, unnecessary loss. The same sad, unnecessary fate awaits many preachers today unless those preachers improve the way they use their voices.

Why would that preacher, or any Christian communicator, willingly abuse his voice? Preachers are in the talking business. So why would a preacher want to destroy or at best minimize the effectiveness of that voice? Some preachers answer that they want to give their utmost to God when they preach; if losing their voice is the inevitable result, then so be it. But how can you give your utmost to God by losing your voice? Some preachers say they do not need speech training. After all, anyone can talk. The issue here is not if a preacher can *talk*, but if a preacher can *communicate*. Effective communication is inversely proportional to vocal abuse. Some preachers are surprised to learn that they can overcome vocal abuse. The good news for all preachers is this: God has equipped us to preach vigorously three or four times a day without suffering a sore throat, hoarseness, or laryngitis. By learning to breathe and speak diaphragmatically, preachers can achieve the full potential of their voices.

The purpose of this chapter is to explain the dynamics of what is called *full vocal production*. Full vocal production enables speakers to preserve and protect their voices. It also enables speakers to realize the full potential of their individual voice quality. There is nothing mysterious about this process. Full vocal production simply puts to use the parts of our bodies that God created for speaking.

Full vocal production is often referred to as diaphragmatic speaking. However, we will use the term *full vocal production* because it better describes the proper vocalization process.

## Diaphragmatic Breathing

Controlled diaphragmatic breathing is intrinsic to full vocal production. (Most speech books refer to diaphragmatic breathing as respiration. However, "respiration" can also refer to breathing that is not diaphragmatic. Besides, I intend my terminology to be descriptive rather than technical.) The primary function of breathing, of course, is to supply oxygen to the body. The speech process depends on this primary function. For that reason, speech is often described as a secondary or overlaid function.

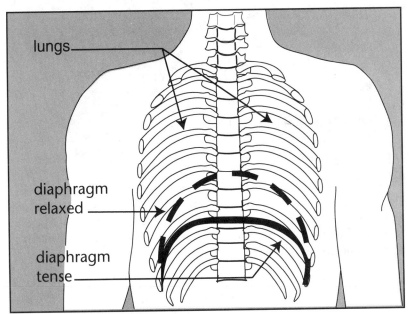

**Figure 1. The diaphragm is tense and flat during inhalation, relaxed and dome-shaped at the end of exhalation.**

Diaphragmatic breathing simply means breathing deeply enough to involve the diaphragm fully. The diaphragm is a thin band of muscle located in the upper abdominal area just beneath the lungs.

The diaphragm separates the chest (thoracic) cavity from the abdominal cavity. The diaphragm is shaped like an inverted bowl or dome with the top of the dome rising toward the lungs (fig. 1). As the lungs are filled with air (inhalation), they expand, pushing the diaphragm downward to a lower, almost flat position. The diaphragm, in turn, pushes the abdominal and rib muscles outward. Inhalation then has been completed.

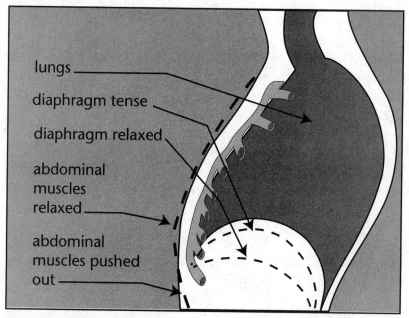

**Figure 2. The downward movement of the diaphragm pushes abdominal muscles outward. The abdominal and intercostal muscles exert pressure on the diaphragm that exerts pressure on the lungs to bring about exhalation.**

In the flat position the diaphragm is tense, much like a compressed spring. The tension is caused by the abdominal and rib muscles, which are returning to their original positions and thus applying pressure to the diaphragm. (Check this out. Take a deep breath and hold it for a few seconds. As you hold your breath, are you holding your lungs? No, you are holding your rib and abdominal muscles so that they will not push against the diaphragm and cause you to exhale.) This tension causes the diaphragm to compress the lungs, increasing the air pressure in them (fig. 2). This compression helps us exhale. The higher pressure in our lungs enables air to move easily from our lungs to the lower air pressure outside of our mouths. (Controlling exhaling, as we will see, is important to full vocal production.) We need to note that in exhaling, the diaphragm returns to its dome-shaped position; it remains relaxed until inhalation forces it downward again and the breathing cycle is repeated.

One can breathe without significantly affecting the diaphragm. This is known as shallow or clavicular breathing because the collar bone and shoulder muscles rise while the abdominal and rib muscles barely move or do not move at all. Shallow breathing has the following devastating effects for the speaker: (1) It deprives the body of an adequate supply of oxygen. The lack of oxygen causes a rapid heartbeat, which compounds the tensions most speakers experience. A sufficient supply of oxygen, on the other hand, helps the speaker relax. Without sufficient oxygen the body weakens, especially the legs. This is the reason nervous public speakers are often described as being "shaky in the knees." (2) The tension produced by shallow breathing is usually felt in the throat and other places. The result is breathiness and a vocal pitch that is higher than normal. (3) The speaker's sinus cavity also closes from tension, and breathing becomes even more difficult. As the speaker experiences breathiness and hears an uncharacteristic stridency or high pitch in voice, a loss of self-confidence occurs. This in turn causes more tension, and the vicious cycle continues until the speaker either relaxes or faints!

Diaphragmatic breathing, then, not only helps the speaker develop full vocal potential, but also provides a way to control tension. All people feel tension or anxiety before they speak; often this is called "stage fright." But tension can be a useful servant to the speaker. When tension is controlled by diaphragmatic breathing, it can be channeled into vitality in the speaker's delivery. (The specifics of channelling tension into vitality in delivery will be covered in chapters 4 and 5.) The first step toward making tension work for the speaker is to acknowledge that tension is natural for all speakers and that it can be modified by diaphragmatic breathing.

## Breathing for Speech

Breathing for speech calls for a simple but special control of the breathing process. Normal or nonspeech breathing is rhythmic: breathing for speech defies rhythm. Stevenson and Diehl describe breathing for speech as having "contrasting rhythm."

> For metabolism it goes like this: Inhale through the nose (1-2-3); exhale through the nose (1-2-3). But in speech it should go like this: Inhale through the mouth (1); exhale through the mouth (1-2-3-4-5-6-7).
>
> Of course, in speech there is no exact mathematical ratio, but when a person is talking he has to inhale quickly and let the breath expire slowly and rather evenly while vibrating the vocal cords. Whereas breathing for metabolism is involuntary, breathing for speech has to be voluntarily controlled.[1]

Many speakers inhale noisily, either because they do not use diaphragmatic breathing or because they feel that noisy inhalation has some dramatic effect. This is unnecessary and distracting. In any speaking situation, some of the air that is inhaled will enter the lungs without any effort by the speaker. A basic law of physics helps the speaker inhale noiselessly. When the speaker pauses for breath, the air pressure in the speaker's body is slightly lower than it is outside the body. Higher air pressure always moves to lower air pressure. Some air, therefore, effortlessly moves into the speaker's lungs. The speaker, of course, must inhale to receive an adequate supply of air. Inhalation does not need to be noisy.

Jon Eisenson, in his superb speech book, *Voice and Diction*, lists three objectives in breathing for speech:

1. It should afford the speaker an adequate and comfortable supply of breath with the least awareness and expenditure of effort.

2. The respiratory cycle—inhalation and exhalation—should be accomplished easily, quickly, and without interference with the flow of utterance.

3. The second objective implies ease of control over the outgoing breath so that breathing and phrasing—the grouping of ideas—can be correlated functions.[2]

These objectives are easily achieved by habitual diaphragmatic breathing.

## Exercises for Diaphragmatic Breathing

Several exercises are helpful in developing diaphragmatic breathing. Here is how to do them.

1. Stand straight, but not rigidly. Place your hands on your sides just above your waist and just below your rib cage. Spread your fingers so that your thumbs point backward and your fingers point forward. Be sure your hands and fingers are touching your body, as if you were trying to wrap your hands around your waist. Inhale and exhale as normally as possible. Your hands should be moved outwardly as you inhale and then fall back toward your body as you exhale. (This will not be a major movement.) If the action is reversed or if you feel no movement, your breathing is too shallow. Repeat the process until your shoulders are relaxed and you are inhaling deeply enough to affect the diaphragm. Remember: clavicular breathing hinders good speaking (and good health).

2. When you have mastered exercise one, add another step to the process. Take a deep breath, then exhale for at least ten seconds. If you are out of breath in less than ten seconds, you are exhaling too quickly. Some vocalists can exhale steadily for thirty or more seconds. Repeat the exercise until you can control how quickly you exhale. Remember, controlling exhalation is critically important for full vocal production.

These two exercises are simple and basic, and there are many variations on them. For example, in the first exercise you could lie on your back on the floor or any hard surface with a book resting on your stomach. The book should rise slightly as you inhale and drop gently as you exhale. For exercise two you could make a hissing sound between your teeth so that you can hear how slowly and steadily you are exhaling. As was just mentioned, some speakers and singers can sustain exhalation thirty seconds or more. This helps them develop strength and versatility with their voices. You may want to invent your own exercises. As with any exercise, you should first take the time to master the basics, and then exercise regularly to maintain the fitness you have achieved.

3. Let's associate diaphragmatic breathing with speaking. Speak the following excerpt from Lincoln's Second Inaugural Address and take a breath where you see the slash marks.

> With malice toward none; / with charity for all; / with firmness in the right, as God gives us to see the right, / let us strive on to finish the work we are in; / to bind up the nation's wounds; / to care for him who shall have borne the battle, / and for his widow, / and for his orphan, / to do all which may achieve and cherish a just and lasting peace among ourselves, / and with all nations.

4. Try the same exercise with this famous passage from Patrick Henry's speech, "A Call to Arms." This time, you mark the manuscript where you feel it necessary to pause for breath.

▼

Gentlemen may cry, "Peace, Peace"—but there is no peace. The war is actually begun! The next gale that sweeps from the north will bring to our ears the clash of resounding arms! Our brethren are already in the field! Why stand we here idle? What is it that gentlemen wish? What would they have? Is life so dear, or peace so sweet as to be purchased at the price of chains and slavery? Forbid it, Almighty God! I know

not what course others may take; but as for me, give

me liberty or give me death!

5. Try this exercise again, but this time, use this excerpt from a Billy Graham sermon:

> Earth never knew a darker day than that first Good Friday, when the Prince of Glory died. But earth's most tragic day was transformed into earth's gladdest day, for it checked the rule of sin over the hearts and lives of earth's people. When Jesus lifted up his voice and cried, "It is finished," he did not mean that his life was ebbing away or that God's plan had been foiled. Though death was near, he realized that the last obstacle had been hurdled, the last enemy had been destroyed, and that he had successfully and triumphantly completed the task of redemption. By his death on the Cross he has removed the last barrier between God and man, and with the words, "It is finished," Jesus announced that the road from man to God was completed and open to traffic.
>
> Shortly after Jesus had uttered those words, his head fell limp upon his chest. A Roman soldier came and thrust a spear into his side and forthwith came blood and water. Physicians say that a mixture of blood and water indicates that he died of a broken heart. But this we do know—that Christ gave the uttermost farthing. He poured out the last ounce of blood to redeem us. He spared not himself. He took heaven's best to redeem earth's worst. Here was the Son of God dying on a cross which was made for the vilest of sinners. Here was the law of substitution raised to the highest degree. Here was the Lamb of God who had come to take away the sin of the world. Here was the blood of God poured out in selfless love for a dying, hopeless, doomed world.[3]

6. Try this exercise with one of your own sermons.

## Proper Vocalization

Full vocal production involves the coordinated activity of several muscles. As we have just seen, diaphragmatic breathing alone involves several muscles and organs. When a person exhales, air moves past the vocal bands (fig. 3). Slight pressure on the vocal bands moves them closer together so that they resist the movement of air. This resistance causes the vocal bands to vibrate. This vibration produces what is called voice (the technical term is phonation). Full vocal production provides a clear, strong voice without the effects of tension or strain.

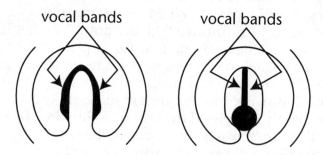

**Figure 3. At left the vocal bands are spread for breathing; at right, they are closed for vocalization.**

Although the process of proper vocalization is not complicated, it is somewhat involved. The muscular coordination needed for full vocal production is much less complicated than would be needed for hitting a golf ball, riding a bicycle, swimming, or other enjoyable, beneficial activities. As with any muscular activity (as we saw with diaphragmatic breathing), full vocal production calls for some concentrated efforts until the basic muscle movements are mastered. Then steady practice is required to maintain good coordination and muscular conditioning.

Let's follow an imaginary molecule of air through the entire vocalization process. A speaker inhales and the air molecule, along with millions of others, is drawn into the lungs. Various chemical changes take place inside the lungs as some oxygen is extracted from the molecule and delivered to the bloodstream. The air molecules are in constant motion, causing the lungs to expand. The diaphragm and the muscles surrounding it are slightly expanded. Almost immediately the muscles surrounding the diaphragm begin pushing back. The diaphragm transfers this pressure to the lungs. (We can temporarily stop this process by "holding our breath." Remember: When we hold our breath, we tighten our abdominal muscles so that they will not return to their relaxed position. This keeps them from exerting pressure on the diaphragm and the lungs.)

The abdominal and rib muscles will be in a hurry to return to their relaxed position. Our imaginary molecule of air will feel this pressure and will be ready for rapid expulsion from the lungs. The speaker who uses full vocal production, however, controls exhalation. This is achieved by controlling the amount of pressure the abdominal muscles are allowed to apply to the diaphragm and thus to the lungs. As the speaker regulates the amount of air that will vibrate the vocal bands, two things are accomplished: (1) the muscular tension for vocalizing is moved from the vocal bands (technically, the larynx) to the abdominal muscles; (2) just as air outside the speaker is vibrated in the production of vocal sound, so the air inside the speaker's lungs is vibrated. This inner vibration reinforces the sound by resonance from the chest cavity. This resonance gives the voice strength and depth. Thus, full vocal production relaxes the vocal bands and strengthens the voice by using the abdominal muscles to control exhalation (and, thereby, vocalization), and thus adds resonance to the voice.

Resonance is defined as the reverberation of any sound. Vocal resonance, therefore, is the reverberation of the voice. Resonance is one of the two most important factors determining individual voice quality. The other is the structure of the vocal bands.

Vocal resonance, or the sound of a voice, is influenced by the chest cavity, the throat cavity, and the nasal passages. The chest is the most powerful of all the resonators, and it is the one resonator that requires controlled muscular activity. The other resonators—head, throat, sinus—influence the voice with little conscious effort. Chest resonance, as we have seen, calls for the coordination of several muscular activities by the speaker. We will discuss this in more detail in the next section of this chapter.

So far, our imaginary molecule of air has been inhaled, forced into controlled pressure from the abdominal and rib muscles and the diaphragm, and vibrated with other molecules of air as they force their way to the vocal bands. Our molecule of air now makes its way past the vocal bands. As it does, it assists in vibrating them for vocalization. Next, the molecule is expelled into the atmosphere to undergo a chemical change that will again make it viable for inhalation. Then the process is repeated. This process was summarized in a classic speech book as follows:

> The foundation of voice is the column of air that is forced out of the lungs by pressure of relaxed diaphragm and rib muscles, and the pressure of the viscera or abdominal organs against the diaphragm in exhaling. The air passes up through the larynx at the top of the windpipe. In the larynx are two muscular folds or bands that in quiet breathing form a V-shaped opening but that pull together when you cough or lift a heavy load. They also pull together when you wish to speak, so that the exhaled air is forced against them. These folds are commonly called the vocal cords—though vocal bands is a more accurate descriptive term. The air pressure vibrates these bands and produces sound waves. The tone thus produced passes through the pharynx (upper throat, where your tonsils are—or were) and the mouth, and, in the case of certain sounds, through the nose. These cavities resonate the tone (literally re-sound it), amplify and enrich it.[4]

In summary, vocalization combines several muscular actions. These activities may appear to be involved, but most of them—breathing and vocalizing—are already in use by the speaker. Full vocal production coordinates these activities so that the speaker may preserve and protect the voice and develop full vocal potential.

## How Do We Get Our Individual Voice Quality?

Individual voice quality is determined by the size and shape of the vocal bands, and by the size and shape of the vocal resonators. Voice quality is as individual as fingerprints. In fact, several court rulings across the United States have allowed voice print identification (spectrograms) as evidence for identification. When the techniques of full vocal production are put into practice, the speaker can get an accurate "reading" of his or her individual voice quality.

The vocal bands are two narrow, tough strips of muscle tissue. They range in length from about 7/8 inch to 1 1/4 inches in adult men, and from about 1/2 inch to about 7/8 inch in adult women. The vocal bands are part of the "voice box" (larynx) at the front of the throat. They are housed inside a protective cartilage that causes a protrusion popularly known as the Adam's apple. The vocal bands are connected in a V-shape and lie flat within the larynx. (See fig. 3.) The opening between the vocal bands is called the glottis.

The length, thickness, and, to some extent, tension of the vocal bands determine voice quality. Short, thin vocal bands produce higher pitched sounds. Long, thick vocal bands produce lower pitched sounds. (Too much tension also produces a higher pitched sound, but full vocal production transfers most of the tension from the vocal bands to the abdominal and rib muscles.) Once full vocal production is used, the speaker should not be concerned about making the voice sound lower or deeper. Full vocal production gives the speaker an optimum or "natural" pitch level. Optimum pitch is largely determined by the size of the vocal bands. The chest cavity, as we noted, provides vocal resonance that gives the voice depth.

## Exercises for Optimum Pitch

You can find your optimum pitch level in at least two ways. (1) Try the breathing exercise that calls for you to lie down with a book on your stomach. When you feel you are breathing diaphragmatically, try vocalizing the sound "ah-hh." Do not whisper the sound; vocalize it. Be sure your throat muscles are relaxed. As your vocal bands vibrate, listen to this sound. It will be very close to your optimum pitch level. (2) Sing the musical scale, starting as low as you can without strain and finish the last note as high as you can, also without strain. Your optimum pitch level will be at about the level in which you sing "fa, sol, la." The speaker should learn to be happy with that pitch level. Many speakers protest that their voices sound "too high pitched." However, forcing the voice lower (retracting the voice) causes damage to the vocal bands. Once the speaker determines optimum pitch level, that level should be accepted as his or her individual voice quality. More often than not, individual voice quality is much more pleasant than the speaker initially perceives it to be.

Do you remember how we traced the route of that air molecule? Vocalization occurs when the stream of breath (millions of molecules) under pressure forces the vocal bands apart. The vocal bands are far apart during breathing, and they are brought close together for vocalization. Air pressure builds beneath the vocal bands until they are forced apart. As the vocal bands are forced apart and air is allowed to pass between them, they vibrate and vocalization occurs. If the air is constantly allowed to pass too quickly between the vocal bands, two negative results occur: (1) vocalization is breathy instead of resonant, and (2) the vocal bands become dry. Speaking when vocal bands are dry is much like driving an automobile without oil in the engine. Dryness causes friction, which does serious, possibly permanent, damage to the vocal bands. (A drink of water gives only temporary relief to the throat and hardly any to the vocal cords.) Full vocal production, with its strong control of exhalation, maintains the "natural" moisture within the larynx. Thus, the vocal bands are protected, and they are allowed to work at maximum efficiency.

The sound that results from the vibration of the vocal bands is reinforced by resonators. The resonators amplify and add further quality to the voice, much as the hollow box beneath the strings adds resonance to a violin. "Resonance gives to the voice greater volume, richness, and penetration: it gives tones a vibrant and bright quality."[5] Resonance occurs in the chest during vocalization, and it takes place in the other resonators just after vocalization. The resonators other than the chest are:

1. The upper throat cavity (pharynx). This is the soft muscular structure just above the larynx that opens into the nasal cavities and the mouth.

2. The nasal cavities, including the nose. Only the sounds *n*, *m*, and *ng* are resonated through the nasal cavity.

3. The mouth. Resonation from the mouth depends on how widely the mouth is opened during vocalization. The size, shape, and general health of the resonators account for their differences in quality for individual speakers.

The way a speaker uses his or her voice can tell much about personality. Speaking (especially preaching) is, in part, an expression of the speaker's temperament. An intense speaker puts stronger emphasis on key words; a deliberate person speaks slowly; a cheerful person usually has a pleasant voice because there is no tension on the vocal bands; a person lacking self-confidence usually speaks in either a quiet voice or in a loud voice designed to disguise the lack of self-assurance; the "loner" tries to escape attention by speaking in a monotone; a domineering person speaks in a lofty, superior way. These are just a few of the psychological qualities of speaking, and they are admittedly oversimplified. Each of us may have several of these qualities, depending on our speaking situation.

## Exercises for Full Vocal Production

If we are to grow as Christian communicators, we must put out a little effort. A few basic exercises will ensure strong, clear voice quality.

1. Standing straight but not rigidly, count aloud from one to ten on one breath. Try to make your vocalization a little louder and stronger with each number. You may want to begin at a vocal level that is a little less than conversational tone. If you make it to ten on one breath, you will discover that the last two or three numbers involve effort from your entire body. (In fact you may be standing on your tiptoes on nine and ten!) If at any point you feel strain or soreness in

your vocal bands, stop! Your voice is a delicate instrument that must never be strained.

Strain on the vocal bands means that you have not shifted the tension from your throat to the abdominal muscles. Concentrate on relaxing your throat muscles and tensing your abdominal muscles during vocalization.

2. Stand straight. Inhale. This time shout the word "Halt!" As you shout, bring your abdominal muscles in with a sharp movement. You should feel as if the abdomen and diaphragm were causing the word to explode from your mouth. This will help you feel what the diaphragm and the muscles around it are doing when you speak with full vocal production.

Do the same exercise using other words, such as "Yea, team!" or "Hey!" or "Watch out!"

3. Try the following excerpt aloud. Speak with urgency, and try to project your voice as if you were speaking in a large room and without the benefit of an amplifier. As always, stop if you feel vocal strain.

> God is not a God of unfinished business. Victory belongs to our God. We are not on a sinking ship. We follow not a blind leader. We serve not a puny God. He sees the end from the beginning, and we need not fear any door to which God holds the key.
>
> This is not a call to complacency but a battle cry. Our God is moving. Let us move with him to victory and immortality, toward the great and terrible day of the Lord.[6]

Notice the short, pungent sentences. Notice the emphatic wording. This is a crescendo of conclusion to a powerful sermon. Try the exercise again, speaking with force. Stop at each punctuation mark, take a breath.

4. Try the same exercise using excerpts from some of your own sermons.

5. Practice controlling exhalation while singing a hymn. Try to control your rate of exhaling while singing so that when you come to a breath-stop in the hymn, you do not need to take a breath. This practice will help you learn to

avoid exhaling too much air while speaking. Again, if you feel any vocal strain, stop! It is never advisable to strain your vocal bands.

6. If you cannot control exhaling from one breath-stop to another during a hymn, you need to develop some basic conditioning exercises. Consult a physician to determine whether you need to jog, ride a bicycle, or do some other exercise. The overall fitness of a speaker is directly related to the ability to communicate strongly and clearly.

Full vocal production is a simple process that requires proper muscular coordination. (It is much more difficult to describe than it is to do!) Using full vocal production will preserve and protect the speaker's voice. Many speakers have done serious and even permanent damage to their vocal bands because of years of vocal abuse. Many other speakers dread Sunday night services because their voices are still sore from the Sunday morning sermons. Some speakers begin to dread speaking at all—not because they don't enjoy speaking, but because they know it will hurt their throats. Other speakers try to compensate by retreating to dramatic whispers during the sermon or by depending too heavily on the amplification system. (What happens when the amplification system does not work? Besides, when we mumble into a microphone, the congregation simply hears an amplified mumble!) Speaking improperly is inexcusable. God has created us in such a way that we can preach two, three, or even four times on Sunday without having a sore throat on Monday.

Full vocal production also helps a person develop the individual potential of his or her voice. A speaker's voice does not have to be, in fact should not be, gravelly and hoarse—unless there is a physiological problem. Speakers should have clear, strong voices, for they have a clear, strong message to proclaim. Most preachers would insist that they and their congregations should give their best to the Lord. Full vocal production is foundational for a speaker to give his or her best whenever speaking. Sermon delivery has been called "the most dynamic moment of the preaching experience."[7] Yet this "most dynamic moment" is often dreaded and then garbled by many speakers. Full vocal production can restore joy to speaking and add dynamism to this "most dynamic moment." Full vocal production is a first foundational step to preaching, teaching, witnessing, and communicating in a way that maximizes the message and minimizes the messenger.

▼

# T W O

*When one who grew up with careless habits as to articulation first attempts to correct them, he will for a while betray the effort; but this can be soon overcome, by practicing exercises in private, and especially by care in conversation.*

John A. Broadus
*A Treatise on the Preparation and Delivery of Sermons*

▼

# Improving Articulation

After full vocal production is achieved, the next step in good communication is clear articulation. Full vocal production, as we have seen, is the foundation of proper vocalization. Vocalization, however, has meaning only when it is shaped into sounds that communicate thoughts. This shaping process is called articulation. The articulated sounds are oral representations of the letters we use in writing. In fact, articulation is to speaking as spelling is to writing.

Do you remember the story from chapter 1 of the preacher who whispered something like "Yeh knee sheeses"? Can you imagine trying to read a sermon with words spelled like that? From many sermons, as they are actually preached, we would be reading something like this: "Doncha wanna cep sheeses? Er yeh gunna say yes to sheeses? Harya wi sheeses, now? Howya lak tuh be wi sheeses? Woncha come? Whaja gunna do?"

Or suppose the Bible were written in the way many preachers speak. We would read something like this from Psalm 23:

Da Lors ma sheper, ah shall not wan
he makes me tuh lah dahn in grain pastors,
he leads me bsahd da still wadders.

Or, from Matthew 16:23: Git thee behind me . . .

Or, while we are having fun, a preacher said, "Ah was so frustrated, I slapped my ford." The congregation pictured the man slapping an automobile. The preacher meant the space between his eyebrows and his hairline.

Or, the preacher who exclaimed, "Mini preachers are causing problems in the churches. . . ." While the congregation tried to decipher whether he meant physical or mental midgets, the preacher knew he meant a large number. Problem was, he did not say many. He said *mini*.

In most cases, the congregation figures out what the preacher is trying to say. But congregations should not have to figure out what preachers are trying to say. The more a congregation has to figure out what the preachers are trying to say, the more the congregation focuses on the messenger, rather than focusing on the message.

Here is a short list of frequently misarticulated words:

| | | | |
|---|---|---|---|
| get | git | think | thank |
| just | jist | thing | thang |
| for | fer | send | sind |
| because | becuz | pen | pin |
| again | agin | ten | tin |
| many | mini | hundred | hunnert |
| our | r | wash | warsh |
| hour | r | naked | nekked |
| or | r | any | inny |
| can | kin | | |

Listen to your own sermons. Can you add to this list?

## Enunciation, Pronunciation, Articulation

The words *enunciation, pronunciation,* and *articulation* are often used interchangeably; one dictionary even defines enunciate as "to pronounce; articulate." For our purposes articulation, as we have seen, refers to the shaping of individual sounds that comprise a word; *enunciation* refers to the overall quality of speech; and *pronunciation* refers to where the emphasis is placed within a word.

The goal of enunciation is much the same as the goal of articulation: clarity of speech. While articulation is concerned with specific speech sounds, enunciation is concerned with the overall quality of these sounds. More often than not, clear articulation leads quite naturally to clear enunciation—but not always. It is possible to articulate clearly, but have, for instance, a muffled enunciation. Try this for yourself. Try saying any of the commonly misarticulated words as brightly and clearly as you can. Next, say these same words, articulating clearly but without opening your mouth any more widely than a ventriloquist. As a result, you will say words like *just, get,* and *for* (and not *jist, git, fer*), but your enunciation will be muffled.

Listen to a brief portion of a sermon you have preached. Listen for some specific trouble sounds. Were they correctly articulated? Was the enunciation clear or unclear? Observe other people when they listen to you. Do they interrupt to ask questions, such as, "What was that last word, again?"

Pronunciation is also important. Correct pronunciation puts the *"em´phasis"* on the correct *"syl´lable,"* as opposed to putting the "em´phas´-is" on the "in-cor´rect syl-la-ble´."

Dictionaries are the best pronunciation guides. Because our language changes constantly and because of regional speech differences (we will discuss accents in this chapter), pronunciation of some words will differ. Here are a few pronunciation problem words:

| | |
|---|---|
| ad´mirable | ap´plicable |
| ce-ment´ | com´parable |
| fi-nan´cial | mis´chievous |
| ex-po´nent | in-sep´arable |
| in´fluence | in-sur´ance |

## Phonemes

American speech uses forty-four distinctive sounds. These individual sounds have the technical name *phonemes.* Phonemes are the distinctive sound elements that, when combined in speech, comprise a word. The different phonemes, articulated correctly, help listeners distinguish words. For example, the pronoun "I" has two sounds: long *i* and long *e.* The word *God* has three distinct individual sounds—the hard *g* sound, the short *o* sound, and the *d* sound.

Clear articulation requires the relaxed, flexible, purposeful use of the lips, tongue, and jaw. That way, the meshing of individual sounds (phonemes) into combinations that form words can occur. The individual sounds of the word *God* are smoothly blended into one syllable, rather than haltingly articulated as three isolated sounds.

When we speak, the sound of the last phoneme of a word is often blended into the first phoneme of the next word. When we say, "God is good," for instance, the individual sound *d* blends easily into the phoneme *i*. This process is called "elision." The elision between the phoneme *s* and the phoneme *g* in the sentence above is not as smooth as it was between *d* and *i*. Try saying aloud "God-is-good" by stopping the last sound of each word before beginning the first sound of the next word. Your speech will be halting and choppy. Elision provides smooth movement so that the individual words are articulated distinctly, but are also blended smoothly into the next word. (In the following chapter we will discuss how pauses are used to interrupt elision, as between sentences.) Clear articulation, therefore, requires distinctive individual sounds eliding in a way that enables the listener to distinguish the speaker's words.

When a preacher has clear articulation, the congregation is free to focus attention on the message. Poor articulation makes listening difficult and transfers attention from the message to the messenger. Poor articulation forces the hearers to focus their attention on deciphering the misarticulated sounds into meaningful words. That is why clear articulation makes listening easy for the congregation.

Speakers misarticulate in three major ways: (1) by substitution of sounds, such as "jist" for "just," "git" for "get," and "fer" for "for"; (2) by omission of sounds, such as "preachin'" for "preaching," "gov'ment" for "government"; (3) by addition of sounds, such as "warsh" for "wash," "athuhlete" for "athlete." As we have already seen, examples of misarticulation are legion.

Most misarticulated sounds are caused by a lazy use of the lips, tongue, and jaw. To verify this, try saying "jist" and then say "just"; say "git" and then say "get." Continue this exercise with the other examples of misarticulated sounds. In each case notice that minimal effort is required to give fullness or clear articulation to these sounds. Failing to put forth even this minimal effort results in lazy or poor articulation.

A few preachers, on the other hand, are overly precise with articulation. The laborious shaping of vowels and consonants also hinders communication, perhaps even more than lazy speech habits. In either case the preacher's goal is to shape sounds so that the congregation can hear the message without the distraction of either lazy or overly precise articulation.

## Pronouncing Proper Names

Residents of some states and cities differ as to correct pronunciation/articulation, and hearers must use their own best judgment to decipher their meaning. Residents of the town of Joshua, Texas, are divided roughly in half as to whether their fair city could be called Josh´uah or Josh´uway. People who live in Missouri disagree as to whether their state should be called Mis-*sour´*ree or Mis-*sour´*ruh. One preacher referred to Mis-*sour´*ree. Later, someone came by to tell him, "Those of us in the know say Mis-*sour´*ruh, not Mis-*sour´*ree." The preacher smiled and asked, "Then, is the state just north of Mis-*sour´*ruh called I-oh-wee´?" The same kind of question could be asked of people in Miami who insist their city should be called Mi-*am´*uh and not Mi-*am´*ee.

Family names, of course, ought to be stated in the way the family prefers.

General acceptance is the best rule for pronouncing/articulating the names of cities, states, rivers, businesses, and streets. Pronunciation guides are published, but not widely marketed. These guides may be found in public libraries. You will want to consult a pronunciation guide for places such as:

Pierre, South Dakota            Metairie, Louisiana
LaJolla, California             Refugio, Texas
Mexia, Texas

## Regional Speech Patterns

Various regional accents may complicate questions of pronunciation and articulation, but they also add flavor to speech. Preachers do well to identify with their people and with their regional accent, but often preachers justify their lazy speech habits by calling them regional accents. Identifying with a regional accent can enhance communication, but lazy speech habits hinder communication. A message from God's Word deserves to be communicated clearly.

Accents are related to both pronunciation and articulation and also include accepted varieties in the rate of speech: slow or fast. Accents represent what the general population accepts for speech in various regions of our country. For example, former President Jimmy Carter's last name is often uttered rapidly and spoken as "Cotta" in the northeastern states; it is drawled as "Cahtuh" in the southern and southwestern states; and it is enunciated as "Carter" in the midwestern and western states. Which is correct? The former president articulates his last name "Cahtuh," reflecting his Georgian speech pattern. It could be argued that "Cahtuh" is the correct articulation of his name because that is the way he articulates it. But a person named Carter who lives in the midwest will sharpen the *r* sounds and articulate the name as "Carter." Would "Carter" or "Cahtuh" then be the correct articulation of that name?

Establishing norms for accents and articulation would be nearly impossible in America. A general rule is this: *The individual speaker does not have an accent unless the speaker leaves the region where his or her pattern is accepted.* Persons from the south, for example, who go to the northeast may be startled by the accent of the persons they meet. But northeasterners will tell them they have a funny accent. Why? Because accents aren't accents in the region where specific articulation patterns are generally accepted.

Speakers who wish to eradicate or modify an accent need especially to evaluate the way they articulate vowels. Consult the articulation guide in this chapter for work on specific speech sounds.

Accents lend color and flavor to speech. Speech would be monotonous without the variety that accents offer. So, be tolerant of the accents of others. Remember that all of us have an accent. We do not recognize it as an accent until we leave our region of general acceptance for speech patterns.

A midwestern preacher spent a year of sabbatic leave in New York City. While riding a subway train from Penn Station to 72nd Street, he opened his New Testament to check a reference in the Book of Philippians. A young man across the aisle observed all this. The young man moved to sit next to the preacher. This is the way the preacher heard the conversation:

"Excuse me, suh, budu know somethin about the Boible?" The preacher, mildly startled, needed just a moment to decipher the question. Then he responded,

"Yes, as a matter of fact, I do. What would you like to know about the Bible?"

"Wool, ah was wonderin', was Jesus a kawpentuh?"

This time the preacher needed a little more time to decipher the question.

"Kaw'pentuh," the man said. The preacher tried to relate the word to a biblical noun, but "Galilean" was as close as he could get, and he knew that was not the answer the young man sought.

The young man sensed he had not communicated. With a tinge of impatience, he said, "Doncha know what a kawpentuh is?" The young man gestured appropriately. "You, know, wi' a hammuh and nails."

"Oh," the preacher finally understood. "Yes, Jesus was a car'penter."

The two men teased each other about their accents. Each thought of the other, *That guy surely does talk funny.*

Accents can be colorful, but lazy speech is a hindrance.

## General Articulation Guide

Study the descriptions of the individual sounds, then say the practice words and sentences aloud. You will find it helpful to practice on a tape recorder.

You may be accustomed to hearing words spoken with sounds different from those indicated in the descriptive list below. Nevertheless, the list gives you each of the forty-four speech sounds, a concise description of how to form that sound in speech, and a few exercise words and sentences that use the individual sounds.[1]

1. Long *a* as in "pay." This sound is produced in the back of the mouth with the middle of the tongue arched and the lips spread slightly.

age  ray  danger

Amos made a plea for a return to the Lord.

The game was played as the evening turned gray.

2. Short *a* as in "sat." The tongue is relaxed, arching the top downward. The sound is formed at the front of the mouth with the mouth opened wider than it was for long *a*. If the tongue is arched and this sound is made too far in the front of the mouth, short *a* will tend to be nasalized. This nasalized short *a* is standard speech in some parts of America.

hat  begat  Acts

Jesus sat and taught them, saying . . .

Andrew and Nathaniel had a visit.

3. *a* as in "father." The tongue is arched back, but otherwise is relaxed. The mouth is open wide as in short *a*, but the sound is formed in the back of the mouth.

calm  palm  ark

The father walked calmly through the dark.

What tall palm tree we saw!

4. *a* as in "wall." The tongue is arched slightly higher than it was for father. The lips are rounded. The sound is formed in the back of the mouth.

5. *b* as in "Baptist." This sound is formed primarily with the lips. The lips are closed, but air behind the lips forces them to open to release the vocalized sound. The explosive part of this sound is usually omitted when *b* is the last letter of the word, such as "comb."

bell  baptize  bless

Brother Bob bought a black suit.

Born again by the blood of the Lamb.

6. *c* as in "Corinth" (identical with *k* as in kite and *q* as in "quick"). This is a nonvocalized consonant. The tongue is firmly arched to the roof of the mouth. The sound is made

as the tongue and soft palate are separated by the compression of air.

care Caiaphas calendar
Calvin commented because he cared.
Caleb called for consideration.

7. *ch* as in "church." This sound is a combination of *t* and *sh*, which we will study later. The front of the tongue is placed firmly on the front part (gum ridge) of the roof of the mouth. The sound is made as compressed air separates the tongue from the hard palate.

child chore chair
Choose to change from teaching to preaching.
The lunch was held in the orchard near the church.

8. *d* as in "do." The top of the tongue is placed firmly against the gum ridge. As compressed air pushes the tongue away from the ridge, the sound is vocalized.

deacon Didymus deliver
The deacon declared his love for the Lord.
Thomas doubted at first but then confessed, "My Lord and my God."

9. Long *e* as in "tree." The tongue is arched to the top, at the middle of the mouth. A little tension of the tongue and lips is required to produce this sound. This sound has various spellings, such as "ski," "believe."

Ezekiel be see
"See Him yonder on Calvary's tree."
Behold, He walks on the sea.

10. Short *e* as in "let." The tongue is slightly arched in the center of the mouth, with little tongue or lip tension.

beget set den
"Lest we forget Gethsemene . . ."
We felt blessed when we met Him.

11. *f* as in "favor." This sound is not vocalized and is produced by putting the lower lip against the upper teeth and forcing air between the lower lip and upper teeth.

fast far faith
The son left the father and headed for a far country.
Find the faith that sets you free.

12. *g* as in "God." This sound is produced like the *c* (*k*, *q*), but there is less tension of the tongue against the palate.

Galatians  garden  Goshen

They gathered in the garden of Gethsemene.

The group grew in spirit and in grace.

13. *h* as in "heaven." This is a nonvocalized consonant. This sound is dependent on the vowel that follows it for its articulation position. The sound is made in the throat almost as a whisper.

half  heard  Hezekiah

Hezekiah heard the prophet as one sent from heaven.

He hallowed the ground on which he humbly walked.

14. Long *i* as in "idol." This sound is difficult to describe. It approximates the sound *a* as in "father" and long *e* as in "he." The sound begins with the tongue in a slight arch and ends with the tongue in a firm arch. The first part of the sound is made in the back of the mouth; the second part is made toward the front of the mouth.

I  pride  Micah

I found the climb to be steep and high.

The light is my guide.

15. Short *i* as in "visit." This sound is produced in similar manner as short *e*, but the tongue is more relaxed and is placed a little lower. The lips are also in a similar position as in the short *e* sound, but they are relaxed.

slip  in  bit

His witness lifted our spirits.

His limited speech was spoken quickly.

16. *j* as in "Jesus." This sound is similar to *ch* except that it is vocalized, and less tension is placed on the tongue.

Joshua  jealous  Jeremiah

The crowd jostled Jeremiah just after he spoke.

Joshua jubilantly joined the battle.

17. *l* as in "Lord." This is a vocalized consonant produced with the tip of the tongue touching the upper gum ridge. The *d* sound is produced in a similar way, but the *d* sound has a stop and the *l* sound is continuous. To accomplish this, the center of the tongue is lowered to allow vocalized breath to pass over the sides of the tongue.

letter learn low
The letter to the churches was a revelation.
The Lord revealed himself to the lonely group.

18. *m* as in "man." This is a vocalized and nasalized sound. The lips are touching, but relaxed rather then pressed together. The teeth are slightly parted, and the tongue rests at the bottom of the mouth. The vocalized sound moves through the nasal passages.

Malachi Matthew member
The members made a major contribution.
We must remember the meaning of the message.

19. *n* as in "neighbor." This is the second of three vocalized and nasalized sounds. The top of the tongue is placed firmly but not rigidly against the gum ridge. The vocalized sound moves through the nasal passages.

Noah near new
Notice that the new book is near your hand.
Noah knew that God had sent the rain.

20. *ng* (or *ing*) as in "preaching." This is the third of three vocalized and nasalized sounds. The back of the tongue is arched and in contact with the soft palate. The vocalized sound moves through the nasal passages.

singing praying bring
He was going to bring a rousing sermon.
Sing a new song of the things which have come to pass.

21. Long *o* as in "chosen." The back of the tongue is arched slightly and the lips are rounded.

owe Obadiah Romans
Don't you know how the song goes?
Moses wrote some of our oldest books.

22. Short *o* as in "cross." The back of the tongue is arched slightly, but is more relaxed than in the long *o* sound. The lips are only slightly rounded.

lost soft wrong
The cost of the office was lost.
He picked up the cloth at the foot of the cross.

23. *oo* as in "doom." This sound is produced with the tongue flattened and the lips rounded. It is a vocalized sound.

room   soon   pool
The book tells of a good man sitting beside the pool.
At noon the world shook and took them by surprise.

24. *p* as in "Peter." The lips are closed, and compressed air behind the lips forces them apart to produce this non-vocalized sound. The lips are much more tense than in the *b* sound.

presence   hyper   Egypt
His parents took him from Palestine to Egypt.
Peter departed to be alone as he wept.

25. *r* as in "religion." This sound can be produced in two ways: with the tip of the tongue arched to the roof of the mouth well behind the gum ridge, or with the center of the tongue arched to the roof of the mouth.

revelation   reverence   career
The preacher rested as he leaned on the rostrum.
The fund raising occurred in October.

26. *s* as in "savior." This is a precise sound that can be distorted easily into a whistling or hissing sound. It can also be made into a sluggish *sh* sound. It is formed via the following articulatory procedures:

a. The sides of the tongue are raised and pressed firmly against the inside of the back teeth.

b. The center of the tongue is lowered at midline, forming a groove.

c. The top of the tongue is placed behind but not touching the backs of the upper teeth.

d. There is a slight space between the rows of teeth.

e. Air is forced along the groove of the tongue toward the teeth.

f. The *s* is a voiceless consonant.
Sunday   Sabbath   sermon
After Saturday comes Sunday.
Sermons are sources of inspiration.

27. *sh* as in "shield." The tongue is flat, and air is forced over the tongue and through the opening between the rows of teeth. The lips are slightly rounded.

shallow should share
The child should share the sherbet.
Shallow sermons do not have sharp points.

28. *t* as in "Titus." The tip of the tongue is raised and pressed against the top of the gum ridge. The front of the sides of the tongue are pressed against the upper back teeth. The sound is made as compressed air forces the tongue away from the teeth.

territory terror table
The Twelve sat at the table.
Two departed and ten were left.

29. *th* as in "thanks." The tip of the tongue is placed between the teeth. Breath is forced between the tongue and teeth to make this voiceless sound.

Thessalonians thanks thimble
Thanks be to the Thessalonians.
The thimble is over there.

30. *th* as in "bathe." This is the same as the *th* above, except that it is vocalized.

soothe scathe either
We loathe the scathing sermon.
He seethed as he bathed in cold water.

31. Long *u* as in "universe." The center of the tongue is arched to the roof of the mouth. The tongue moves to a flattened position as vocalized air moves past it. The lips are slightly rounded.

music mute humor
The music was heard on cue.
Humor in the Bible is unique.

32. Short *u* as in "usher." The tongue is relaxed, but the center is arched a little and the mouth is open without rounding the lips.

under utter asunder
Under the leadership of Ahab, the nation suffered.
The city was utterly destroyed and torn asunder.

33. *v* as in "victory." The *v* is produced much like the *f*, with these exceptions: the *v* is voiced and is produced with less air pressure.

valid  visit  veil
The veil of the temple was divided.
It is valid to make a pastoral visit.

34. *w* as in "will." This sound has two movements: initially, the lips are rounded in pursed position but not touching the teeth. The tongue is arched in the center against the soft palate. The lips spread slightly at the end of the sound. This is a vocalized sound.

wisdom  was  winsome
It was his will that he speak wisely.
The winsome widow seemed aware.

35. *wh* as in "whither." This sound is produced just as the *w* is produced, except *wh* is not vocalized.

where  which  whether
When you decide whether to go, let us know where.
Which do you prefer, white or blue?

36. *y* as in "yield." The center of the tongue is arched toward the front of the mouth against the hard palate, and the lips are spread slightly—almost in a smile. This is a vocalized sound.

yesterday  yes  yonder
Yom Kippur was observed yesterday.
Yes, you may yield.

37. *z* as in "zealot." This sound is produced in the same way as the *s* sound, except the *z* is vocalized and the *s* is not. The *z* is produced with less tension on the tongue than is the *s*.

zoo  Zacchaeus  Zipporah
Zipporah felt Moses was zealous.
Zacchaeus seized the opportunity.

38. *zh* as in "treasure." *zh* is produced in the same way as *sh*, except the *zh* sound is vocalized.

azure  brazier  seizure
The seizure occurred under the azure sky.
The treasured writing was thrown into the brazier.

39. *dzh* as in "wages." This sound is similar to the *ch* sound, except that it is vocalized.

wages  ages  stage
The stage was set for Jonah.
The wages of love last for ages.

40. *a* as in "task." This sound is placed after the others because it is rarely distinguished in American speech. Because of its regional quality, I recommend you master this sound only if you plan to work in the New England area, or in areas where the spoken English bears a British influence. This sound is between the *a* sound of "sat" and the *a* sound of "father."

Because of regional differences, any word exercises here may not be distinguishable to some regional speech patterns. Therefore, they are not included in examples 40–42.

41. *o* as in "coffin." This is another regional sound that is not generally distinguished in America. This sound is produced much like the short *o*, except the lips are rounded.

42. *er* and *ir* sound. There are a variety of regional practices for producing this sound. For some speakers, the *r* sound suffices, for other speakers there is a distinctiveness between the *r* sound and the *er-ir* sound. This sound is produced in similar fashion as the *r* sound except that a little more tension is put on the tongue, and the lips are not rounded.

43. *ou* as in "thousand." This continuous sound is generally produced with the tongue arched to the back of the soft palate. The lips are spread slightly and move to a rounded position.

    rouse  pout  round

    The round man was aroused to anger.

    A thousand soldiers were routed in battle.

44. *oi* as in "soil." This is a combination of the sound for *o* as in "coffin" and the long *e* sound as in "tree." It is a continuous vocalized sound.

    turmoil  avoid  toil

    They toiled in the oil fields.

    The turmoil was avoided.

A careful study and practice of the sounds indicated here will help the speaker improve articulation. The benefits will be more clear and therefore more easily understood speech, enabling the audience to concentrate on the message, not the messenger.

▼

# T H R E E

*I have heard of a brother who in his earlier days was most acceptable, but who afterwards dropped far behind in the race because he by degrees fell into bad habits: he spoke with a discordant whine . . . and used such extraordinary mouthings that people could not hear him with pleasure. He developed into a man to be esteemed and honored, but not to be listened to . . . .*

*Doubtless, faults in even so secondary a matter as posture have prejudiced men's minds, and so injured the success of what would otherwise have been most acceptable ministries.*

Charles Haddon Spurgeon
*Lectures to My Students*

▼

# Improving Vocal Variables

An elementary rule of communications states that a speaker's emotional message is more quickly conveyed than the intellectual message. The emotional message involves the feelings—authority, love, resentment, and others. The intellectual message involves the words used to communicate the message. The intellectual message deals directly with language, while the emotional message is sometimes categorized in a vague field of study called "paralanguage."

The preacher's emotional message should support the intellectual message. The relation between the two can be illustrated by the various uses of the word *no*. We can say "no" tentatively in a way that says, "Keep on asking and I will change my response." We can also say "no" thoughtfully in a way that says, "I am not totally convinced that my response is correct. I am open to new information." Or we can say "no" obligingly in a way that says, "I don't want to say 'no,' but I feel I must." And, we can say "no" definitely in a way that says, "My negative answer is final!" The intellectual message remained the same in each response, but the emotional message was completely different in each case.

Communication experts do not agree about what constitutes paralanguage, nor about what we have referred to as the emotional message.[1] Some scholars include only the vocal variables—pitch, volume, rate, and pause. Other scholars would include only *body language*—posture, gestures, facial expressions, and personal appearance. Since both the vocal variables and body language are intrinsically involved in effective communication, we will discuss both of them.

We will consider each of the vocal variables in speaking: pitch, volume, rate, and pauses.

## Pitch

The first vocal variable, *pitch*, refers to the tonal qualities produced in vocalization. As we saw in chapter 2, vocalization is produced as a controlled breath that is exhaled past the vocal bands and vibrates them. All vocalization is produced at various pitch levels, ranging from high to low. Five factors need to be understood in our study of pitch: optimum pitch, pitch range, pitch interval, pitch intonation, and pitch inflection.

1. *Optimum pitch* was discussed in chapter 1. The optimum pitch level is the median level from which higher and lower pitch levels develop.

2. *Pitch range* refers to the span between the speaker's highest and lowest pitch levels. A wide pitch range, used effectively to support content, gives a speaker flexibility and enhances communicative appeal for an audience or congregation.

3. *Pitch interval* refers to the distance between two consecutive pitch levels. A change in pitch level can occur between two words or within one word. A pitch interval within a word is often heard in the word *welcome*. The first syllable is usually said a little higher than the second if the speaker wants to communicate warmth and enthusiasm. If a speaker wants to be formal in saying "welcome," each syllable will be uttered at the same low pitch level. No pitch interval will occur.

Pitch intervals between words can be experienced in quoting the first five words of Psalm 23:1. "The Lord is my shepherd. . . ." With a pitch interval between "the" and "Lord," the word *Lord* stands out.

4. *Pitch intonation* refers to the pitch range used within a certain group of words such as a phrase or a sentence. If

pitch intonation repeats itself frequently, a pattern can be easily detected. Later in this chapter, we will look at several examples of intonation problems, including a monotonous pattern.

5. *Pitch inflection* refers to the movement from one pitch level to another within a syllable or a word. Use of inflection was illustrated in the opening paragraphs of this chapter, when several uses of the word *no* were given. Varieties in pitch inflection were used to modify the emotional message.

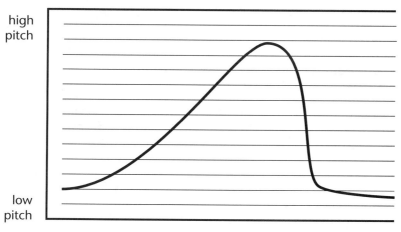

high
pitch

low
pitch

"I'm so glad you are here to worship with us t–o–d–a–y."

**Figure 4.**

Pitch inflection patterns involve predictable ways of inflecting or intoning a sentence. One of these ways has become known as "the ministerial tone." I find it so offensive, however, that I've decided to call it "the ministerial whine."

This pitch pattern is illustrated in figure 4. Here we need a machine that has not been invented. This machine would follow the same principle as an electrocardiogram, which measures the depth and rhythm of the heartbeat. The machine would type the words of our sermons and record the pitch variations used with the individual words. In lieu of this uninvented machine, I submit a rough sketch. The horizontal lines indicate the range of pitch. Notice the definite pattern of the ministerial whine.

Multiply this pattern over hundreds of sentences in a thirty-minute sermon, and you can easily recognize why a rescue mission congregation would turn down a warm meal rather than endure a sermon preached in ministerial whine.

Another pitch pattern problem for preachers involves the last few words of sentences. In this pattern the concluding words are spoken with a predictable drop in pitch (see fig. 5). This is usually done for two reasons: (1) some preachers feel this is the only way to let the congregation hear something they cannot see, that the sentence is ending; and (2) the speaker is thinking about the next sentence and subconsciously allows the energy level to drop. Such preoccupation causes the pitch pattern to look similar to figure 6 (see following page).

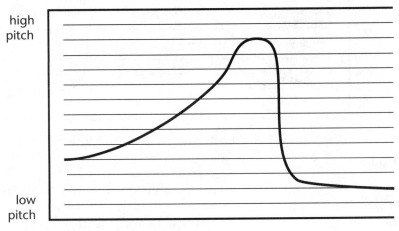

"I hope you receive a real b–l–e–s–s–i–n–g."

**Figure 5**

## Exercises for Pitch

How can you avoid monotonous pitch patterns? By relating the use of pitch to content! Try typing a transcript of one of your recent sermons from a tape recording. (A transcript differs from a manuscript in that it is a copy of what has actually been said, whereas manuscript is a copy of what was planned to be said.) Copy the sermon word for word from a tape recording. Be honest in transcribing. When "git" is said in "Git thee behind me, Satan," then transcribe it g-i-t.

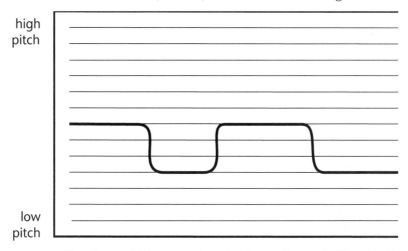

"Read your Bible every day. Study God's word diligently."

**Figure 6**

This transcript will help you to see and hear the sermon simultaneously.[2] Listen for pitch patterns. When you detect pitch patterns, stop the tape. Use the transcript to say the same words aloud, this time striving to relate pitch to content. You may need to experiment several times to develop an ear for your own pitch patterns. You may need someone to help you detect any pitch patterns. Further exercises for all of the vocal variables will be discussed in chapter 5.

Using a transcript has been the best single corrective exercise I have ever used to improve content and delivery. The tediousness of transcription repays itself richly with the excitement of discovering ways to improve delivery immediately. The transcript approach is time-consuming and humbling. After the first exercise, it may be sufficient to transcribe only a few paragraphs rather than the entire sermon. Remember, your goal is to use pitch in a way that supports your content.

Your preaching may also suffer because you use only a narrow range of pitch. When you do this, all words tend to sound alike. Because the transitions and descriptions do not stand out, your congregation has difficulty following your message. The narrow pitch range may be graphed in this way (fig. 7).

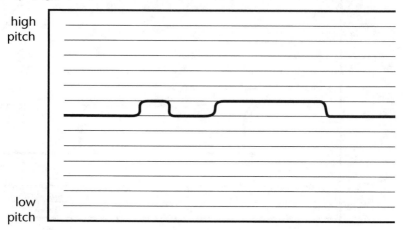

"Read your Bible daily. Study God's word diligently."

**Figure 7.**

Preachers who have a narrow pitch range usually think they are using a much wider range, and they feel their message is being communicated clearly. Often such speakers feel that if they use a wider pitch range they will be too demonstrative or dramatic.

To solve this problem, you may need to do a little psychological reconditioning. One way to accomplish this is to use a practice tape recording in which the speaker uses a much wider variety in pitch than would ordinarily be used in oral communication. The purpose of this exercise is to remove the inhibitions that limit the use of effective variety in pitch. For the inhibited speaker, a good communicative pitch range may "feel" demonstrative and dramatic. By exaggerating the use of pitch, one may open the door to effective changes in speaking. Emphasize variety in pitch inflection.

The process goes something like this:

▼ Listen to a portion of a recent sermon while looking at its transcript.

▼ Turn off the recorder and iterate the same words, using exaggerated variety in pitch.

▼ Repeat the exercise.

▼ Record on another tape the same portion of transcript while striving to use a wider (but not exaggerated), more effective range of pitch.

▼ Compare the practice tape with the sermon tape.

▼ Repeat the exercise until you feel comfortable using effective variety in pitch.

Remember, your goal is to use pitch to support content. Keep on asking yourself, "How can I say this in a way that the congregation will understand and feel the message I am trying to communicate?"

Also try this exercise with excerpts from sermons of other preachers. Read the following excerpts aloud. On the first reading, deliberately use a monotone. On the second reading, use a wide pitch interval. Exaggerate your inflections. For the third reading, use pitch as effectively as you can to communicate effectively.

The major hindrance in our relationship with God is due to the lack of spiritual elevation in our lives. Anyone who has ever flown in an airplane is aware of the view from the higher perspective. Or, if you have seen the view from the top of the Sears Tower you realize the difference. And so it is in our relationship with God. We must elevate our thinking, our minds, and our attitudes to a higher, spiritual plane. The advantage of elevation allows a broader range of vision, a better view, and a different insight. Once our minds are elevated, seeing and knowing God take on a new meaning.

———

Our prayers are evidence of what we expect God to do, but many really do not expect to commune with God. That is why it is very difficult for God to get our attention. You have heard the story over and over, but I will tell you once more just to remind you (certainly in light of the flood situation this past week) about the man who had been praying to God to rescue him because there was a flood and his house was covered with water.

He sat on the roof and as the water began to rise, a helicopter came by, and the pilot said, "Come on up, we are going to rescue you," but the man answered, "No, no, God is going to rescue me," and so the helicopter flew away. The man continued to pray and next, a motorboat came by and the captain said, "We came by to rescue you," but the man replied, "No, no, God is going to rescue me." You know the story, the water came up and the man drowned.

When he reached heaven and began to complain to Peter, he said, "Look, Peter, I should not have died because I prayed and waited on God to rescue me, but He didn't rescue me and now I am dead—I died because God didn't come to rescue me." God answered and said, "I sent a helicopter by for you and you refused it; then I sent a boat by for you and you refused that." Often we are like that man. When God sends us a lifeline, and it does not meet our expectations, we refuse what He sends. But Isaiah expected God to commune with him and was greatly blessed thereby, for God revealed to him His holiness.[3]

▼

The next excerpt is primarily narrative. Again, do the monotone, the exaggerated, and the effective reading. On the third reading, concentrate on using pitch to communicate that you are quoting a monologue.

His face was drawn, more troubled than I had seen it before. It framed two haunted, deeper-set eyes than normal. His need was obvious.

"I feel so left out of it. My family would prefer me dead. My business has practically folded due to intrigue on my partner's side of the firm.

"The firm is not firm—and neither am I. I cannot honestly say that I have one true friend on this planet. I even fondled my thirty-thirty rifle last Monday with the first stages of premeditated self-murder in my mind."

"How deep is your loneliness?" I asked, probing clumsily.

"As the sea . . ."

He knew and I knew that his depression was so deep he was bathing in despair.

At this point I felt Satan's subtle whisper, "Now, don't quote Scripture to him—that's the last thing he needs." But I proceeded to tell him I was preaching the next Sunday on the most encouraging verse in the Bible.

"God knows, I could stand a lot of that," he said, wistfully.

"Would you like to see how a pastor prepares a sermon like this?"

"Yeah, sure—you're going to show some of the tricks of the preaching trade?"

"No tricks, not even clean ones—just straight digging until the Bible gold vein is found; then you yell 'Eureka.'"

I read the verse I considered the most encouraging verse in the Bible, Hebrews 13:5b, "I will never leave you nor forsake you."

Now, this is either a bland sentence, or it is God's solid gold.

We must dig deeply into this rock to see what it yields. We must ascertain the answers at least.

1. What does *never* mean?

2. What does *leave* mean?

3. What does *forsake* mean?[4]

▼

The next excerpt calls for solemnity and somberness of expression. Do the three readings as you did with the first two excerpts. Work to use lower pitch effectively on the third reading.

In this touching passage is more than a tremendous word of advice. It is an admonition and a commandment.

Brethren, if a man be overtaken in a fault, ye which are spiritual, restore such a one in the spirit of meekness; considering thyself, lest thou also be tempted. Bear ye one another's burdens, and so fulfill the law of Christ (Gal. 6:1–2).

Do you know someone who used to walk with the Lord but who is not close to Him now? All through this message, think of the person who has been ambushed and sabotaged by the devil and who has fallen into sin and disrepute. They are broken, discouraged and in the bondage of guilt.

Once that person loved God with all his heart, all his mind, all his soul, all his strength, but now he is a broken brother or a broken sister. Image that person in your mind, and even now begin to pray for that broken one.

Our Scripture is about God giving to us a ministry of restoration. Let us ponder this ministry which is imperative from God's standpoint.[5]

▼

## Volume

Volume refers to the amount of force needed in speaking for the message to be heard and for the emotional message of the sermon to be conveyed. Preachers have the same problems with volume as they have had with pitch: narrow range and monotonous patterns.

The most obvious problem related to narrow range is the use of excessively high volume. Too many preachers have been misled by the fallacy that preaching is acceptable only if it is loud. (Narrow ranges of volume may, of course, occur at any level—high, medium, or low.) The answer is to realize that volume is a servant of content. Volume should support the message. Volume should not be known simply as the trademark of the messenger. The speaker should therefore use force or abstain from it as *content* dictates.

Two typical volume patterns are heard frequently in preaching. One pattern has high volume at the beginning of a sentence and low at the end of a sentence. Some preachers think this downward slide gives the congregation a vocal signal that the sentence has ended. The preacher knows the congregation cannot see the "period" at the end of the sentence. Lower volume (accompanied by a brief pause) is the signal the congregation needs. But this soon develops into a predictable and distracting volume pattern. The preacher should experiment with differing volumes throughout the sentence (as dictated by content), especially at the beginning and end of the sentence. This graph represents what happens when volume is up at the beginning of a sentence and down at the end (fig. 8).

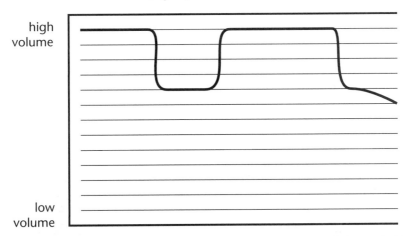

"Read your Bible every day. Study God's word diligently."

**Figure 8.**

The other common volume pattern is the dramatic whisper. This results because of the widespread notion that the preacher must shout throughout the sermon. Most preachers are not strong enough to shout for that long. They need some breaks. Often the break from shouting is a retreat to the dramatic whisper. In any case, the result is a pattern in the use of volume that magnifies the messenger instead of the message. The next graph illustrates the use of this kind of volume pattern (see figure 9 on following page).

Even if a preacher has the physical strength to shout throughout the sermon, the preacher would be using a limited volume range. His dubious goal would be to have volume level at the top of the scale throughout the sermon, and the graph would look like this (see figure 10).

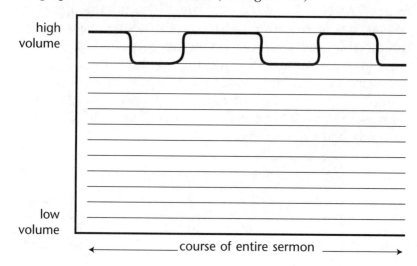

**Figure 9**

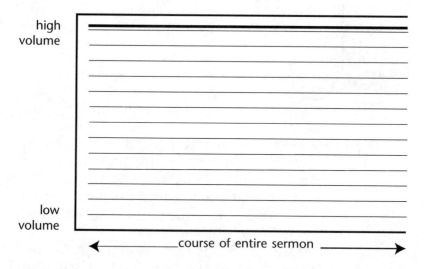

**Figure 10.**

Note that this limited volume range indicates that all of the content should receive equal emphasis. That means that illustrations would sound as emphatic as key theological assertions. Imagine a preacher thundering out, "JESUS

HONORS THE FAITH OF A REPENTANT SINNER!" That may be worth shouting about. But if this shouting preacher is to meet the goal, "THAT REMINDS ME OF THE TIME I WAS A LITTLE BOY!" must also be said in a thundering voice. The theological assertion and the personal illustration, according to this preacher's use of volume, are of equal importance. The illustration, of course, is not so important as the theological assertion and should be given less emphasis by using lower volume level. In that way, volume supports content.

Some preachers react to this approach by a determined effort to avoid "preacherly" high volume. They are prone to make a similar mistake, however, by using volume in a narrow, low range and again without strong relationship to content. Their use of volume is easily graphed (fig. 11).

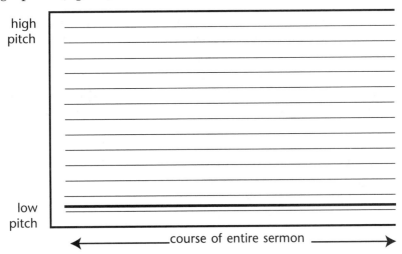

**Figure 11.**

Many preachers use volume in a narrow but medium range that also does not relate strongly to content (see figure 12 on following page).

When pitch and volume are used effectively to support content, graphing is without pattern and difficult to illustrate.

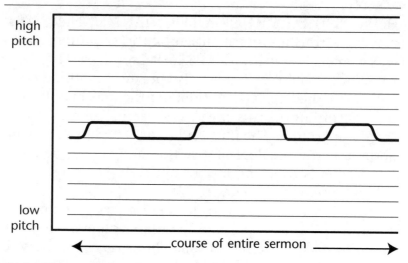

**Figure 12.**

### Exercises

Again, it helps to prepare a transcript of a recent sermon. You can achieve variety in volume much the same way you practiced achieving variety in pitch; exaggerate the use of higher or lower volume as needed.

We may use the same kind of exercises for volume as you did for pitch. Read aloud the following excerpts. First, read at the shouting level of volume; second, read at a low-level monotone, but not a dramatic whisper; then, use variety in volume as effectively as you can on the third reading. The first excerpt calls for lots of variety in volume.

> And if that person will not respond, but becomes stubborn, hard to reach, set in his opinions, believes he is right in his own mind, and doesn't want to come in communion again with his brother or his sister, then you have no recourse but to bring it to the church and let the church know what is going on.
>
> Do you know what the Bible says the church should do? When the church hears that several ways have been tried to bring the brother into the fold and he refuses, then Jesus says outright, the church should declare that person as if he had never been saved. Oust him. Now, in the New Testament Paul writes two letters to a church that had been playing

with sins of different kinds, and in his first letter to the Corinthians, chapter 5, we read of some conditions under which churches should act in that regard.

We read 1 Corinthians 5:9: "I wrote you in my letter not to associate with immoral people; I did not at all mean with the immoral people of this world, or the covetous, and swindlers or with idolaters, for then you would have to go out of the world," and go to the moon, "but actually I wrote to you not to associate with any so-called brother if he should be an immoral person, or covetous, or an idolater, or a reviler, or a drunkard, or a swindler, not even to eat with such a one," don't even invite him to your house. Cast him aside. Cut his membership, he is no longer a member of your church.[6]

▼

The next excerpt will call for emphatic volume in several sentences.

With great joy I am glad to be able to tell you that He is the conquering Christ. In the ninth verse, the Scripture says, "And immediately the man was made whole, and took up his bed, and walked." Back of every command Christ gives, He places His divine omnipotence. To say it in another way—He never orders anything He can't pay for. When Jesus gives a clear command, we have only one adequate response: Do it!

Notice the contrast with Jesus and the would-be "healers" of today. No suggestion that the man wait in a "prayer line." No suggestion that he send in a "free-will offering." No suggestion that he order a "prayer cloth" or "healing oil"—just the instant divine mandate to be healed. The full compliance of all forces and powers were at the Savior's command. What a wonderful thing to say to a sin-sick, sin-cursed, ailing, hurting, bleeding humanity—Jesus is the conquering Christ!

You may be faced with a challenge today, and you say, "I can't." Oh, yes you can! You may have received a challenge to start a new church, to build a new class, to witness to a friend, and your response may be, "I can't." Oh, yes you can! You can do anything your Savior has asked you to do.

Let's let this picture of the compassionate, challenging, commanding, conquering Christ totally dominate our lives for Him![7]

▼

The next excerpt calls for a medium level of volume.

Two years ago William Henderson lay sick in bed. His jaw was swollen from the infection of a decayed tooth—or so he believed. The only medication being administered was pain-relieving aspirin. Uneasy because of the presence of fever, his mother called the doctor. To the surprise of William and his mother, the doctor quickly asked a question, 'Have you stepped on a nail recently?' In his astonishment the boy simply pushed his foot from under the sheet and displayed to the doctor a small but angry-looking puncture in his instep. The doctor promptly gave William a shot and by quick and radical action was able to save him from death by lockjaw. An uncritical mind had confused symptoms with disease, and only drastic and prompt action prevented death.

Such an uncritical diagnosis in the sphere of spiritual and moral life has often confused the symptoms of sin with sin itself. In an effort to treat some of the symptoms of sin, many have confused sin with intellectual ignorance and have prescribed education as the panacea. This attitude may be seen in the early philosophers of Greece as well as in the latest writings of crass rationalists. Others have interpreted sin in a sociological context, and by manipulation of the environment have attempted to treat the symptoms of sin that stand like open sores on the body of humanity. More recently, some have identified sin with psychological frustration and have looked to adjustment as the proper answer. But ignorance, squalor and frustration are only symptoms of a deeper causative factor in human experience.

The Bible makes plain that sin is fundamentally spiritual anarchy. Its symptoms may vary with circumstances, but the essential nature of sin is in the realm of the spirit. Paul concluded his exposition of the meaning of sin and grace in the Book of Romans with a grand summary statement that the wages of sin is death, but that God's gift is eternal life in Christ Jesus (Rom. 6:23). The very words used by Paul in this bold statement of fact speak eloquently of the nature of sin, not in definition but in description of its dire effects upon human life.[8]

▼

## Rate

*Rate* refers to the speed at which a person speaks. Rate is misused in three ways: the speaker talks too fast, too slow, or at the same rate throughout. A flexible rate is best. The content should determine how much your rate varies. Use a faster rate for the less important details; then slow down for key assertions and ideas. A very slow, deliberate rate, with a minimum of elision, gives strong emphasis.

Many preachers think they must speak rapidly in order to communicate excitement. But rapid speaking is only one way, and not necessarily the best way, to achieve that goal. All of the vocal variables, as well as the use of body language, should work together to communicate varying levels of excitement.

Some preachers insist that it is "natural" for them to speak rapidly or slowly. But what does this have to do with nature? In any case, the misuse of rate calls attention to the messenger rather than the message. The purpose of speaking is hampered when the audience notices how rapidly or slowly the preacher is talking. Rather than becoming a servant to rate, fast or slow, the speaker should make a servant of the message.

### Exercises

Several good exercises can help control rate. Reading aloud the poetry of Walt Whitman or Robert Frost virtually defies rapid speech. Care must be taken to paint the same oral pictures they have drawn verbally. Even so, the rate will vary. Examine the following excerpt from "Drumbeat" by Whitman.[9]

| | |
|---|---|
| Slow, emphatic: | beat! beat! drums! |
| | blow! bugles! blow! |
| Slightly faster: | Through the windows— |
| | through doors— |
| | burst like a ruthless force, |
| | Into the solemn church |
| | and scatter the congregation. |
| | Into the school where the scholar is |
| | studying . . . . |

Try this passage from Scripture:

| | |
|---|---|
| Slow: | "Saul, Saul, |
| Moderate: | "Why are you persecuting me?" |
| Fast: | And he said, |
| Slow: | "Who art thou, Lord?" |
| Fast: | And He said, |
| Moderate: | "I am Jesus who you are persecuting." |

Rate has many variations. "Slow," "moderate," and "fast" are mere guidelines. Most people use a wide variety of rate in normal conversation, but they tend to become inhibited in public speaking and speak at the same pace.

The best method for correcting problems in rate has already been prescribed. Examine the transcript of a recent sermon while listening to it on tape. As you look at each sentence of the sermon, ask why that particular rate was used. Select key passages in the transcript and experiment with a variety of rate levels. Determine which is best for that particular passage.

As a basis for self-testing, think of 125 to 150 words-per-minute as average. This pace allows little room for variety. For this average you can increase your variety; a little faster than 150 words-per-minute at times when sermon content does not require special emphasis and a little slower than 125 words-per-minute when sermon content does require emphasis. Consider a few excerpts from the sermon, "The Prophetic Ministry," by G. Earl Guinn.[10] The opening paragraph may be read at 100 to 125 words-per-minute:

> When our ancestors were drinking blood out of the skulls of their forefathers on the shores of the Baltic Sea, China and India were ancient civilizations. They were religious countries then, and they are the same today. Their cultures have been more or less static and constant. In many respects they were not unlike the ancient Egyptians, Persians and Hebrews. They took worship seriously, even to the point of sacrificing their offspring to their deities. Now our Western civilization and culture stand aghast at the fiendish fetishes of the ancient rites. We have differing standards and concepts of value. Whence came this difference? For the most part the difference is due to the views of and efforts of the prophets of Israel. Never in the history of the race have so many owed so much to so few. Jesus was in the line and tradition of the Hebrew prophets, although far more than a prophet. To the Christian he is Son of God and Redeemer. Yet many of his pronouncements were prophetic. He came not to destroy the law and the prophets but to vindicate, enrich and make complete.

▼

The last paragraph of the introduction might call for a slightly faster rate—perhaps 125 to 150 words-per-minute:

> In the Boston public library there is an impressive painting of John S. Sargent showing these men as living characters. It would be helpful if every preacher had a copy of this painting hanging on the wall of memory to remind him always that his primary task is the preaching of God's truth. There is a call today for the prophetic type of ministry.

The conclusion to this sermon, as we have already noted, is a crescendo, and it defies rapid rate. Each sentence is an assertion that must be emphasized. Read a portion of that conclusion aloud, timing yourself as you do. Try for a rate of 90 to 110 words-per-minute:

> Listen, men of God! Are you in his will and cooperating with his purpose? Are you serving his cause and preaching his grace? Then stop worrying about your opposition and pay no attention to their looks. God Almighty is marching on. He who notices every sparrow's fall and holds the whole wide world in his hand will never leave thee nor forsake thee. Let the heathen rage and the wicked imagine a vain thing. He will have them in derision. He that sitteth in the heavens shall laugh.
>
> God is not a God of unfinished business. Victory belongs to our God. We are not on a sinking ship. We follow not a blind leader. We serve not a puny God. He sees the end from the beginning, and we need not fear to enter any door to which God holds the key.
>
> This is not a call to complacency but a battle cry. Our God is moving. Let us move with him to victory and immortality, toward the great and terrible day of the Lord.

▼

Remember, use variety of rate in a way that supports content, and not in a way that calls attention to the speaker.

## Pauses

Rate and *pauses* work together. When rate and pauses are discussed together, they are usually known as phrasing. In oral communication, a phrase is a group of words expressing a thought. These phrases are separated and at the same time interlocked by pauses. To communicate our message effectively, we must use pauses in a variety of ways.

*Brief pauses* are used to allow the listener time to absorb what is heard. Longer pauses usually indicate a change of thought, but they may also be used to increase the attention of the congregation. Intermediate pauses may be used to introduce or dismiss a related but extraneous idea, to make a transition from one thought to another, or to allow time for descriptive material to be absorbed.

Follow this general guideline: a brief pause is about one second or less in length; an intermediate pause is one to two seconds in length; a long pause is three to five seconds in length or longer. As with rate, there are many options for the lengths of pauses.

*Short pauses* are appropriate in reading Matthew 5:13 because of the relatedness of the material: "You are the salt of the earth;" (short pause) "but if the salt has become tasteless," (intermediate pause) "how will it be made salty again?" (short pause) "It is good for nothing any more," (short pause) "except to be thrown out and trampled under foot by men" (NASB).

*Long pauses* are most often used to indicate a change of thought. They are also good devices for gaining attention. The lengthy silence (lengthy, that is, when compared to the brief and intermediate pauses that are used most of the time in preaching) draws attention to itself and thus to the next few words you preach. Use a pause for this purpose infrequently, and only when you have something very important to say. As your sermon progresses, you may need an occasional long pause when you move from one point or section to another. The long pause allows time for information to be digested, and it communicates the fact that a major shift in ideas is taking place. Consider an excerpt from the sermon "The Gospel of Isaiah" by Herschel H. Hobbs.[11] The first point is "The Gospel Concerning Sin." The second point is "The Gospel Concerning Suffering." Note the need for a pause:

> Only when we stand in the searching presence of the righteousness of God in Christ Jesus do our own righteous efforts appear as filthy rags. Thus even our noble attempts at self-salvation, spawned in unbelief, become sin (John 3:18). It is in this light that Isaiah regards men. This is the message of the gospel concerning sin.

[Intermediate to long pause, perhaps two to three seconds].

Every moment we live testifies to the truth that sin produces suffering. While a given pain is not necessarily traceable to a given sin—although it may be—it is true that all suffering and death are attributable to the evil which is resident in the universe and in men's hearts (Gen. 3:3, 16–19). Paul sums it up in one phrase, "The wages of sin is death" (Rom. 6:23). The conclusive proof of this truth is seen at Calvary.

*Intermediate pauses* have numerous uses and are of varying lengths, depending on the demands of the content. When Jesus said, "Behold, there went out a sower," an intermediate pause is needed after "Behold." The word *behold* means, "let me have your attention," or "listen to this." In this instance, an intermediate pause allows time for attention to be focused on the words that follow. A similar pause may be used to introduce a quotation. For instance, "his mother said, 'Whatsoever he saith unto you, do it'" (John 2:5). The intermediate pause is needed between "said" and "Whatsoever" to indicate that the quotation is about to begin. Intermediate pauses are also effective at the end of assertions or quotations, because they allow time for the congregation to absorb the message. Punctuation marks are good indicators. They are not fool-proof, but they can be helpful in pausing/phrasing during sermon delivery.

Vocalized pauses are all too common. Sounds such as "uh" and "er" and "yuh know" communicate a feeling of uncertainty. A few vocalized pauses may be acceptable to most congregations, but they carry no intellectual message and they diminish the preacher's sense of authority or credibility. Be especially aware that vocalized pauses can become an unconscious habit—unconscious, that is, to the speaker. The congregation will notice them quickly. I once counted eighty-two "uhs" in one twenty-minute sermon. Do not be afraid of a silent pause; a silent pause is much more effective than a nonsensical vocalized pause.

### Exercises

Take the sermon transcript you have already used for pitch and volume. Listen for the pauses. Were they vocalized or silent? Were they of appropriate length? Did the pauses support the content?

Experiment with pauses. Choose a passage in your transcript where you made an emphatic statement. Read the passage aloud. On the first reading, pause for about seven seconds before your most emphatic words. On the second reading use no pause at all. On the third reading, use pauses as effectively as you can.

Do the same three-readings process for the following excerpts. The first excerpt calls for several intermediate, and some lengthy pauses.

> Three words in English, one word, *tetelestai*, in Greek—this is the greatest word ever spoken about Jesus and his vicarious and substitutionary death on the Cross. Yea, it is the greatest word uttered in the greatest moment of time by the greatest Person who ever trod this earth. That word expresses the greatest fact concerning the greatest number of people, bringing the greatest blessing to the greatest multitude in earth and in heaven—a multitude no man can number. That one word in Greek expresses the greatest single triumph in the history of the human race.
>
> "It is finished!"
>
> That statement shows that the hope of humanity is no longer a dream. Spoken on earth's most transcendent day and in the most climactic moment of that day, those words of redemption show that all the prophecies and promises made by God were now sealed, completed, and accomplished.
>
> That redemptive statement is infinity flung into three words, a fortune in one jewel, a volume in three words, an oratorio in one statement, an ocean in a cup, all organs in one diapason.[12]

▼

The next excerpt calls for several brief, and some intermediate pauses.

> I have been asked to speak upon the subject announced: "America's Number One Health Problem— Alcoholism." This is a subject in which the men of

the clergy and the men of surgery should be profoundly interested and concerned. No two groups in American society have a graver responsibility or a greater opportunity to do something constructive about the growing evil of alcohol than the men of the ministry and the men of medicine.

———

The challenge is to all of us as men and women of God, as professional leaders in our communities, as individuals of unusual privilege and opportunity, as mothers and fathers and Christian leaders, as followers of the compassionate Great Physician, Jesus Christ, the Man of Galilee. The challenge is to us to consider the whole problem, the vast scope of it, the millions of lives that are affected by it; to consider the possible downfall of our own nation because of it; to refuse to be deluded by subtle catch phrases and propaganda clauses; but courageously to take our stand and hold it always for total abstinence, for that which builds up and never tears down, remembering we are indeed our brother's keeper![13]

▼

Volume, pitch, pauses, and rate are all servants of content. When these vocal variables are used in ways that do not support content, they call attention to themselves. This impedes the effective communication of the sermon. Effective use of full vocal production and the use of vocal variables in a way that supports content, emphasizes the message rather than the messenger.

▼

# F O U R

*There is no easier way to disrupt communication than by awkward or poor use of the body. One of the regrettable incidents of preaching occurs when the minister delivers two sermons—one with words, and another with the body.*

Brown, Clinard, Northcutt, and Fasol
*Steps to the Sermon*

▼

# Improving Body Language

Nonverbal communication, more popularly referred to as *body language*, includes these factors: personal appearance, perceptions gained by the congregation in their first impressions of the speaker, walking to the pulpit or lectern, eye contact, facial expressions, posture, and gestures. These visible communication signals either support or hinder the message being expressed through language and voice. Body language communicates a message without saying a word. In preaching, body language should support content.

In fact, we would have difficulty communicating through language and vocal expressions alone. Try speaking without body movements. The vocal variables tend to be flat or in a narrow range. This is true whether you suppress gestures by making your body tight and rigid, or by making it extremely relaxed. *The communicative act requires the use of the total body.* The act of communication rarely depends solely on the speech and breathing mechanisms.

Just as the communicator has difficulty speaking without body language, so the listener has difficulty receiving a message without body language. Body language helps a preacher induce a sense of empathy. Notice how football fans tense their bodies and push as if they were actually carrying the football those last few yards into the end zone. Notice how they imitate the "high fives" and the gyrations of the players when the touchdown is made. Using body language, a speaker may communicate urgency, intensity, resignation or excitement. This enhances the impact of the message on a listener. "Whenever an audience participates with the speaker, feels with him, yields to his movements, the speaker is well on the way toward achieving his purpose."[1] Body language augments preaching. Listeners respond better to a message from a person with whom they are involved. Body language that supports content dramatically helps produce that involvement.

## Personal Appearance

The role of personal appearance in the communication process will never be known exactly. Too many variables occur in the tastes, subcultures, generation gaps, and individual idiosyncracies that shape the way a listener perceives a mode of dress. "We do know, however, that appearance and dress are part of the total nonverbal stimuli which influence interpersonal responses—and under some conditions they are primary determiners of such responses."[2]

Most preachers are expected to wear a suit and tie. While there is tolerance for the preacher shedding the coat, and loosening the tie, at least the first appearance by and the first impression of the preacher is one of full decorum. This conveys an impression of respect, perhaps reverence, for God by dressing at one's best. Formal dress emphasizes the seriousness of the occasion, without totally disallowing opportunities for some informality, some fun. Casual dress is interpreted as emphasizing the informality or fun of the occasion, but not totally disallowing opportunities for some serious expressions of worship.

The only general rule to apply regarding appearance is sensitivity. The speaker should dress for the occasion, whether it be informal, formal, or somewhere in between. The speaker's dress should never distract the congregation from the message. A speaker can be distracting both by overdressing (too many colors; too formal for the occasion) and by underdressing (too informal for the occasion). The speaker should ask, "How will my appearance affect the way my congregation perceives me as a person?" There may be no single accurate answer, but these considerations may minimize possible distractions.

## First Impressions

Obviously, personal appearance plays a significant role in developing a first impression. Beyond that, however, the congregation will also judge the potential of a speaker by personal grooming, by the way the speaker meets others, and the speaker's apparent comfort level for the speaking opportunity. The speaker's goal is to communicate self-assurance and ease that falls well short of arrogance but well above self-rejection.

## Walking to the Pulpit

Listeners continue to gather information as they observe the way the speaker approaches the moment of delivery. The congregation has already been responding to the cues the speaker gives through personal appearance. This impression can either be affirmed or denied by the walk to the pulpit. The preacher's goal is to communicate alertness, self-confidence, and eagerness to share a message.

Take note of how people walk toward something that interests them. They do not walk on their toes. They do not slouch. They are not rigid. A natural movement to the pulpit informs the congregation that you are comfortable and happy to be their speaker. (Consequently, it is unnecessary to open the sermon with mundane remarks such as, "I am so happy to be here today," nor is it necessary to begin with an amusing anecdote that serves no purpose in that particular speaking situation.)

Heed this related piece of advice: do not speak before reaching the pulpit. The speaker should be established at the pulpit or lectern before one word is said.

## Eye Contact

Make eye contact immediately. This is an excellent way for the speaker to become established at the pulpit before uttering the first word. Eye contact may be the last step in first impressions. Please observe three major concerns about eye contact:

1. *Establish eye contact before you speak the first words.* Look toward the eyes of the congregation. There is no need to "nail" anyone with an intense gaze. Some persons will feel that you are looking directly at them, even if you are only looking in their general vicinity. Do not look over the heads of the congregation. Look directly at the people, and, without moving too rapidly, establish eye contact with most if not all of them.

2. *Maintain eye contact during 75 to 90 percent of the sermon or lesson.* You should be so familiar with your notes or manuscript that you have no obvious dependence on them. Especially, never look down at your notes during or at the end of a key statement. This is a common mistake. When you have something important to say, maintain strong eye contact. Glance at notes during the pause after you complete the statement.

3. *Maintain eye contact while turning pages of your notes or manuscript.* Don't be conspicuous when you turn the pages. Use small pages or cards, or slide the pages aside rather than turning them.

## Facial Expressions

You can communicate an amazing variety of emotions through your facial expressions. This may be the most direct means for a congregation to "read" you. As with all areas of delivery, your facial expression should suggest, enforce, and support content. Never use a smile when a frown is appropriate—or vice versa. Imagine a preacher forcefully speaking about the need for a loving attitude while glaring at the congregation! Or a preacher commenting on Paul's emphasis on joy in the Book of Philippians with a sad or expressionless look.

What does a facial expression look like to a congregation? Most preachers have no idea. They do well to avoid the superficial and overly dramatic, but they are ignorant of facial expression. A videotape can help them see what the congregation saw at the moment of delivery. When they watch a videotape, most preachers recall having felt intense emotion, but they are surprised that these emotions did not show up in their in facial expression. You may have this experience. *There is often a gap between what you as the speaker feel and what you actually communicate.*

The best exercise for closing the gap between feeling and expression is to exaggerate your various facial expressions. For instance, try smiling, and look in a mirror while holding the smile. If you see little if any smile in the mirror, broaden your smile. You may feel that the smile is too broad, but you may see in the mirror the smile you only felt was there before. This exercise helps you as a speaker coordinate what feels like a good smile with the amount of muscular activity required to produce that smile.

The best facial expressions occur when the speaker is rid of inhibitions. The best facial expressions unconsciously reflect the speaker's emotions and feelings.

Try reading the following excerpts aloud. For the first reading, frown heavily. During the second reading, smile brightly. On the third reading, try to let the content dictate your facial expressions. The third reading of this excerpt should call for a pleasant expression on the first paragraph, and a serious expression (but not a frown) for the remaining paragraphs.

> The Sunday evening worship service was over. At home the children finished their good-night snack and sleepily dressed for bed. It was the four-year-old's turn as the family knelt for prayer. Suddenly, wide awake now, he lifted his tousled head to say, "Mommy, what is the cross?" That night the preacher had preached about the cross of Christ, and even amid twists and turns and space ships and rocket guns drawn across the face of the bulletin, the four-year-old had heard enough to innocently inquire, "What is the cross?"
>
> The Bible has much to say about the cross of Christ. It speaks of the physical instrument of torture upon which Jesus of Nazareth was put to death. It tells of lonely anguish, judicial mockery, and brutal shame. There was a jeering mob and the click of dice in quest of a robe; there was blinding pain and torturing thirst; there were curses, nails and blood. All this

is included when the Bible says simply, "And they crucified him" (Mark 15:25).

But it says more!

It is immediately apparent that the physical cross, in all its grim reality, points beyond itself. It is the broad picture window through which we can behold the suffering heart of God laid bare before man's sin.

The Bible says of Jesus that it pleased God "to reconcile to himself all things, whether on earth or in heaven, making peace by the blood of his cross" (Col. 1:20, RSV). The apostle Paul declared that the main purpose of his ministry was to proclaim the good news of salvation, but "not with eloquent wisdom, lest the cross of Christ be emptied of its power. For the word of the cross is folly to those who are perishing, but to us who are saved it is the power of God" (1 Cor. 1:17–18, RSV). Concerning the motive for his life's activity, Paul exclaimed, "Far be it from me to glory except in the cross of our Lord Jesus Christ" (Gal. 6:14, RSV).[3]

▼

A pleasant facial expression is appropriate on the third reading of the following excerpt.

The father receives tenderly when we return. The father kissed him tenderly or covered his face with kisses. Even more than in our world this was a sign of forgiveness and restoration to relationship. After Absalom had rebelled against David, his father received him back this way (2 Sam. 14:33). God wants to demonstrate outwardly and obviously His tender reception when we return to Him.

The father does all of this before the son says a word. This means that there is nothing in God that should cause us to hesitate in coming back. There are no grounds for reluctance regardless of what you have done or how long you have been gone.

God reacts with eagerness when we come back. The word "quickly" should not be ignored. The father does not even let the son repeat his memorized and rehearsed speech. God does not investigate or humiliate when we return. He interrupts the carefully crafted speech of the son with showers of honor and festivity. What God does for us He does quickly.

God reacts with generosity when we return. None of the things done for the son was in the order of a necessity. He could have come back on probation. He could have been received with reserve and coldness. He could have been welcomed with a sedate, private ceremony. But the Father gives more than enough. Salvation is more than mere pardon and an embarrassed reception back into the family. It is justification, sanctification, adaption, responsibility in the church, resurrection, and glorification. God does more than the necessary when He saves.[4]

Try this same approach on your own transcript. If you have a videotape, observe how you used facial expressions in relation to content.

## Posture

The guidelines for good posture are more flexible than the guidelines for any other area of public speaking. In all areas of communication, individual differences are as numerous as individual speakers. This is especially true of posture. Each speaker should determine the most comfortable way to stand in order to communicate eagerness and self-confidence. Good posture for speaking is neither rigid nor slack. It simply provides a comfortable position for vocal communication and other forms of bodily expression. Therefore, a posture should be chosen that assists the smooth movement of head, arms, and torso.

The position of the feet is intrinsic to comfortable posture. Again, you must determine which angle and space between the feet is comfortable. Look for a position that helps you shift the body smoothly to the front, back, or either side. For instance, you may move one foot forward and then put most of the body weight on that foot. This causes a slight leaning toward the congregation and communicates a sense of urgency. Conversely, putting most of your weight on the back foot communicates a sense of rejection or withdrawal. You should work through your message and determine beforehand which of the various postures you should use. As always, posture and its changes should support content.

Beware of shifting weight from one foot to another. This is one of the chief distractions in the use of body in speaking. Your congregation will perceive this shifting as a swaying motion. Body swaying is usually done rhythmically and is almost always the result of unchanneled nervous energy. This swaying motion occurs when the feet are side by side. When body sway is a problem, the speaker should correct it by placing one foot slightly forward and placing most of the body weight on the forward foot.

### Exercises

*Exercise #1.* Use the transcript of your sermon. Speak the words first with your body weight on a back stage foot. You will be leaning away from the congregation, communicating a sense of withdrawal or rejection. On the second reading, stand with your feet side by side; avoid a swaying motion. This stance communicates a sense of neutrality. On the third reading, put weight on your forward foot—half-a-shoe-length forward may be enough. This communicates a sense of urgency, conviction, and intensity.

*Exercise #2.* Read the following excerpt in all three stances. Which stance do you think is more appropriate for this excerpt?

The root of sin is unbelief of God's unfathomable love. God's effort to save the prodigal has been to make his heart known. As a last resort, He sent His only begotten Son to reveal His bleeding heart to today's "Adams and Eves." The cross of our Lord is the supreme revelation of God's bleeding heart for us. His heart broke; and He bled to death for a prodigal like myself.

What should be our response to such a loving God? We do magnify Him; we enthrone Him as the Lord. Is that all? No! We rise to join with another forgiven prodigal who said, "Now I rejoice in my suffering for your sake, and in my flesh I do my share on behalf of His body in filling that which is lacking in Christ's affliction" (Col. 1:24).

The forgiven prodigals do not merely glory in the Christ crucified. They take up their crosses to participate in His suffering. Many Korean Christians bled and died in His name.

To take up the cross is to join in the suffering of our Lord in seeking the prodigals. The cross-bearing is an essential sign of His disciple. I believe God of Genesis 1–3 demands this just as our Lord lovingly demanded His disciples.[5]

*Exercise #3.* In the following excerpt, determine when there is occasion to use the stance of withdrawal, the stance of neutrality, and the stance of conviction.

Bitterness is the fruit of an unforgiving heart. We must therefore never allow our disappointments in others to canker into resentment by harboring them in our hearts. We must rise above resentments at all costs. We must remember the best and forget the rest. If we spend our time trying to get even we will never get ahead.

But how do we do that? Is it possible for us to really forgive those who let us down and disappoint us? Yes. Yes, it is. There is a way. It is by God's grace.

Just as it did with Paul, the grace of God that flows from Calvary to our hearts can enable us to rise above the disappointments and hurts of life and pray for those responsible for them. This grace to forgive is one of the ways God helps us.

Let the judges judge. Let the prosecutors prosecute. Let the juries condemn. You forgive and pray for those who hurt you. Never let the failures of others make you bitter or a quitter. God's grace will enable you to do that. That's one of the ways He helps us.[6]

One possibility for using posture to support these would be to put your weight on the back foot during the first reading, sustain a neutral stand during the second and third readings, and put your weight on the forward foot during the fourth reading.

## Gestures

Good gestures are impulsive, but they are also well-timed and well-coordinated actions of the entire body. To simplify discussion, we will consider gestures only as they relate to the hands and arms.

Few of us talk without using our hands and arms. Most speakers who do not use gestures have been carefully taught to resist the natural impulse to do so. Gestures can be a valuable asset to the speaker if they are used spontaneously to support content.

Using your hands when speaking is not necessarily an undignified way to communicate. A wife watched her husband describing a key play from the previous night's basketball game. His expression was animated, and his description mesmerized his listener. The speaker's wife interrupted him in midsentence to ask, "Can't you speak without using your hands?" The speaker paused with hands and arms frozen in midair in the gesture he was using before the interruption. With hands and arms still in the same position, he turned to his wife with a quizzical expression on his face and asked her, "Why would you want to?" Precisely.

Gestures should be impulsive reflections of the speaker's feelings. When they are, they support and assist language and vocal expression.

Gestures must be timed to mesh with language and vocal expression. Timing is especially important in emphasizing a point. It would be ludicrous to make a vocal emphasis and then pound the pulpit two seconds later! Gestures must be timed to support content.

Gestures must be coordinated smoothly with other communicative actions. If an emphatic statement is to be made, facial expressions should reflect concern, posture should communicate urgency, and gestures should be emphatic. The body should work as a well-coordinated unit.

Yet most speakers feel self-conscious about gesturing. If we think about how to use our hands, we become conscious of them, and this leads to inhibitions. That is why the best gestures are spontaneous and unplanned. If a speaker is having difficulty obeying the impulse to use gestures, a few simple exercises will help.

### Exercises

*Exercise #1.* Do you tend to pin your elbows to the sides of your body? Most inhibited communicators do this, and it results in inadequate, half-arm gestures. If this is your problem, try the following exercise routine:

- ▼ Stand in an open area.
- ▼ Move the right arm across the body, with the arm nearly parallel to the floor.
- ▼ Move your arm until it is extended all the way to the right in a slow, sweeping motion. Note that the elbow was not pinned to the side.
- ▼ Repeat the same exercise with the left arm.
- ▼ Next, use both arms at the same time, just as a football referee would signal an incomplete pass.
- ▼ These exercises will help you break the inhibition of moving your arms past the center line of your body. (This imaginary line is about the same vertical position as the spinal cord. Some speakers unconsciously develop an inhibition against moving their arms past that imaginary line.)

*Exercise #2.* These exercises will help the speaker feel comfortable about using full-arm gestures.

- ▼ Lift the hands, palms up, till the arms are just above a line parallel to the floor. Palms up indicate acceptance. To communicate rejection, stand with the elbows at the sides and hands perpendicular to the floor.
- ▼ Push the arms forward as if an object were being shoved out of the way.
- ▼ With the hands next to the shoulders and perpendicular to the floor, move them until the palms point down and the arms are parallel to the floor.

*Exercise #3.* Use your transcript to practice gestures. If you have a videotape of yourself, observe how you used gestures in relation to content.

▼ Try to recite from your transcript without using any gestures.

▼ Use expansive, exaggerated gestures on the second reading.

▼ Use gestures as effectively as you can to support content on the third reading.

*Exercise #4.* The following excerpt requires lots of support from gestures. Try reading it first without gestures, then with exaggerated, melodramatic gestures, and finally, with gestures that support content. Feel free to try gestures you may have never used.

And the King was deeply moved, and went up to the chamber over the gate and wept! And as he went, thus he cried: "Oh, my son Absalom, my son, my son Absalom, if only I had died in your place. Oh Absalom, my son, my son!" (2 Sam. 18:33).

And thus is the unclaimed love of a father, like a great diamond Star of India, exposed in the window of a pawnshop. A treasure of vast value made cheap, even lost.

It is the parable of the prodigal son dying in the pigpen far from the father who would have embraced and loved him. And what is the sin of the elder brother in this Old Testament parable? Not bitterness but apathy.

God alone grieves the loss of rebels! Apathy—who comforts a king when a rebel dies? No one much. They saw only the rebel's long hair and remembered his Bolshevism. But not the king! He wept. Apathy—it bakes casseroles for church fellowships while battles rage in the woods of Ephraim. And turnpike-wide, they drive forward like lemmings into hell. Churches don't cry. Seminaries don't cry. Book stores don't cry. Only God cries!

But they are lost—perished and gone!

But not just lost. Not just perished in hell, but hanging in the tangled thickets of life, trying in their last moments or first to make meaning of it all. Waiting for a kinder Joab who can weep with God. We shoot our wounded, too—Joab-like in the thickets of Ephraim.

Drugs, booze, the cancer ward, the divorce courts—*the cities themselves are the thickets!* And God weeps and waits, and Jesus, levitating from Olivet, cries out, "Into all the world . . . ."

Please care, please care, please care.

Don't take a plan of salvation—
or any other plan.

Take me, the dying Christ,
and get to the hurting world before Joab does!
    For they hang in tangled woods
with tangled minds.[7]

▼

Be careful that gestures do not become distracting. If you use too many gestures, your listeners may see only a flurry of motion. Rhythmic gestures draw attention away from the message; these are any repeated movements that appear to be in tune with some inaudible beat.

## Summary

Body language should always support content. Body language supports content by reinforcing the vocal variables or, at times, by communicating a message that is not or cannot be communicated orally. Vocal variables and body language work spontaneously and harmoniously to support content. They should not sound or look staged, and their use should by synchronized.

Hercules Collins, an eighteenth-century English pastor, concluded a section of his chapter on "Ministerial Gifts" with sage advice on the deportment of the minister and management of voice:

Let your Carriage and Habit in a Pulpit be grave and sober, let us have no indecent Behaviour, no uncomely Garb. . . . We must speak so loud as our Auditory may hear us, or else both the End of Preaching and Hearing is lost. And to be uneven in our Voice, to be sometimes very high and loud, and then presently very low, the former part of the Sentence may possibly be heard by most or all, but the latter part may not be heard by a sixth part of the People; so that they had almost as good heard nothing, if they cannot hear the whole Sentence. How is the End either of preaching or hearing answered in this? Isa. 58:1 Lift up thy Voice like a Trumpet. . . . And take heed of an affected Tone in preaching; let your Voice be natural, or else sound Doctrine may be liable to Contempt.[8]

▼

# F I V E

*Bible reading offers the widest scope for the enrichment of public worship and it is a great pity that the Scriptures are often so badly read.*

*When the Book is well read . . . it can do for [the people] what sermons often fail to do: it can be the very voice of God to their souls.*

W. E. Sangster
*The Approach to Preaching*

▼

# Improving
# Oral Interpretation

Full vocal production, clear enunciation, and the effective use of vocal variables and body language are interrelated. We have treated them separately only for purposes of analysis. Oral interpretation integrates these speech disciplines.

Oral interpretation is both a science and an art. As a science, it requires hypothesis, analysis, experimentation, and a tentative application. As an art, it calls for physical and vocal expressions with shades of meaning and feeling as determined by the interpreter (artist).

*The scientific process* involves an analysis of the literature (or precepts as in a sermon) to be communicated. The nature and purpose of the literature to be communicated must be determined by linguistic, lexical, historical, and spiritual hypotheses, analyses, experiments, and applications.

*The artistic process* involves the subtle shading of physical and vocal expressions. These expressions are shaped by the integration of full vocal production, clear enunciation, and versatile use of the vocal variables and body language into effective, interpretive communication. Oral interpretation, therefore, is the process that "puts together" the varied speech functions for effective communication.

A good technical definition of oral interpretation describes it as *"the process by which a reader, communicating from a manuscript through vocal and physical suggestions, stimulates a listener response that is favorable to the reader's judgments of the intent of the literature.*"[1] Christian communicators must consciously study God's Holy Word. Our interpretation must be as biblically centered as we can possibly suggest it.

Oral interpretation, then, involves *literature*, a *reader* who suggests the meaning of the literature, and *listeners* who follow the suggestions of the reader. We will expand this definition as we apply it to preaching. Thus, for our purpose, the term "literature" will include not only material written by someone else (for example, the Bible), but will also include the manuscripts, notes, or extemporaneous messages from which sermons are preached. "Reader" will be expanded to include not only the person who reads a portion of Scripture or other literature, but also the person who publicly speaks a message (such as a sermon or devotional thought). We do not need to expand the definition of "listeners."

In Scripture reading, we have these elements in the oral interpretation opportunity:

Bible ⟶ Bible Reader ⟶ Congregation

If oral interpretation fails, the fault could be with the reader or with the listener. While we can do little in this book to assist listeners, we can do a lot to prevent the failure of the reader.

A similar situation exists for preaching/teaching or any other opportunity to communicate a Christian message. We have:

Sermon/Lesson ⟶ Preacher/Teacher ⟶ Congregation

In both cases we seek not only to say the words but also to communicate what we feel. Therefore, we should seek to communicate what the congregation should feel when those words are spoken.

*Suggestion* is a key word for understanding the oral interpreter's task. Suggestion falls short of dramatizing the message but moves well beyond the mere utterance of words. The oral interpreter attempts to suggest the meaning, the ethos (the emotional qualities) of the message in a way that brings the listeners to an identical or similar level of understanding. That is, the listener should experience the same feelings the preacher feels and intends to communicate. For example, the oral interpreter who wishes to suggest an attitude of *agape* (the Greek word for self-sacrificing love) must use physical and vocal expressions that suggest *agape*. Frowning and fist clenching, for instance, are not appropriate. "The oral interpreter works with the listener rather than performing for the listener. The oral interpreter suggests, and if his focal and physical expressions are vivid and accurate, the listener will be able to fulfill those suggestions in his own mind."[2]

*Dramatizing*, as opposed to suggestion, calls for extreme involvement by the speaker. If you were reading from Matthew 5, for instance, you would speak as loudly in an enclosed auditorium as Jesus did on the mount in the open air. If you were describing the emotional agony of King David, you would fall to the floor or lift your hands to heaven or stamp your feet and cry, "Absalom, Absalom, O my son Absalom . . . . " in the way you assume David did. Dramatization is appropriate for a dramatic monologue or in theater presentation, but suggestion is more suitable to a worship service.

Merely speaking words is less satisfactory than suggestion, perhaps even less satisfactory than dramatization. The speaker who uses a monotone or a narrow range of vocal variables together with placid body language communicates a disdain for the message. This is true whether one reads the message or preaches/teaches from notes or extemporaneously. Again, suggestion is far superior to just mouthing the words.

Unlimited variations do occur in individual speaker styles and abilities. Therefore, no specific warning signals can be given to advise when a speaker has gone beyond oral interpretation to dramatization (or, for that matter, when the speaker has achieved good oral interpretation from the lower level of mere utterance of words). However, some general guidelines can help the speaker become more effective in reading and speaking. These guidelines presume a working knowledge of full vocal production, clear enunciation, effective use of the vocal variables and body language, and the ability to express one's self language in a clear manner.

Our general hypothesis is this: good oral interpretation combines speech and linguistic skills in a way that maximizes the message and minimizes the messenger.

## Public Reading

1. Determine beforehand the nature of the literature to be read. Ask yourself: What type of literature is this? Is it poetry, such as Psalm 23? Is it history, such as Joshua 24? Is it wisdom literature, such as Proverbs or Ecclesiastes? Is it apocalyptic literature, such as the Book of Revelation?

2. What is the setting? Is it public oration, such as the Sermon on the Mount? Who is speaking? Who is listening? (As an example, understanding Jesus' audience helps the interpreter of Luke 15.) Why are they listening? Is it temple worship? Private conversation? Questions such as these will lead to an understanding of the meaning or purpose of the passage.

3. Distinguish the supporting ideas from the main idea of the passage. The author will usually explain, expand, or amplify the main idea. The speaker should not overemphasize these supporting ideas, unless there is some specific purpose for doing so. For instance, the phrase "he humbled himself" in Philippians 2:8 supports the imperative, "Let this mind be in you, which was also in Christ Jesus" in Philippians 2:5. Verse five, then, should receive more emphatic suggestion than verse eight.

4. Determine the proper word groupings. As we have seen, the grouping of words between pauses in speech is known as phrasing. Punctuation marks are important, but they may not always be the best determinants for oral phrasing. Phrasing can support the true intent or meaning of a text, or it can distort the meaning of a text. Notice how changes in the phrasing change the meaning of this passage (the slash marks represent pauses).

And I / said the Lord / must be high and lifted up.
And I said / the Lord must be high and lifted up.
And I said the Lord must be high and lifted up.

The first version indicates the Lord is the source of the quote. The second version indicates the speaker is the source of the quote. The third version, spoken without a pause, indicates that the speaker is the source of the quote, and the lack of a pause suggests the quote is not to be taken seriously.

## Experimental Stage

Make a preliminary determination as to which words and phrases should be emphasized. Remember that vocal emphasis is achieved by inflecting pitch a little higher on a specific phrase, word, or syllable. For example, without changing volume, say the following questions aloud with higher inflection on the fourth word: "Is that story *really* true?" Try a passage of Scripture, this time emphasizing the personal pronoun by using inflection: "Sir, what must *I* do to be saved?" Try a conversational phrase, this time inflecting every word: "Hi, son, Get in, let's go." Say the same words again, this time using no inflection. The first greeting sounded cheerful because of inflections; however, the second greeting sounded solemn because of a lack of inflection.

Try this slight paraphrase of John 2:5, emphasizing only the capitalized words:

"AND Mary said / whatsoever he says to do /
you do it."

The emphasis on the conjunction is obviously misplaced. Read the passage aloud again, this time emphasizing the next word:

"and MARY said / whatsoever he says to do /
you do it."

The emphasis on "Mary" is helpful, but strong emphasis is not necessary, since she has already been identified in the preceding verses. We will skip the word *said* in the exercise and try the emphasis on the next word:

"and Mary said / WHATSOEVER he says to do /
you do it."

This reading makes much more sense than the first two. Continue this exercise through the end of the sentence. Notice that each time the emphasis is changed, the meaning is altered. In reading the Scriptures, be certain to place the emphasis on the words and phrases that call for emphasis.

The degree of emphasis should be varied throughout the reading. Some passages may have no words or phrases that need major emphasis. Other passages may have words and phrases that call for varying degrees of major and minor emphasis. In still other passages, only one or more words should receive strong emphasis.

Look for transitions. A transition may be as brief as a single word: *moreover, therefore,* or *however.* (The words *well* and *now* are weak words for transition purposes, and are grossly overused by preachers.) Transitions may also be phrases, such as "on the other hand." Or transitions may be complete sentences: "We have seen that Jesus is divine. Next, we will see that Jesus is also human."

Transitions are expressed by combining inflection, pause, and body language. "The voice may convey a transition by change from a fuller to a lighter tone, or from a quick tempo to a slower tempo, or the reverse. It may change from a major key to a sad, melancholy key or from a staccato to legato movement. You may indicate a transition by a slight shift of the body, a change of posture, or a movement of the head."[3]

Contrasts involve the presentation of opposites. The use of contrasts can deepen the emotional experience. Jesus used contrasts: "You have heard it said, 'an eye for an eye, and a tooth for a tooth,' but I say unto you . . . ." Paul also used contrasts: "The wages of sin is death, but the gift of God is eternal life through Jesus Christ our Lord." Contrasts can best be expressed by variations in pitch level, pitch inflection, volume, and rate. Experiment with these word variables and, as always, strive for oral interpretation that supports content.

## Application Stage

The final step in adapting oral interpretation to speaking is to bring all of the preceding steps together. Try to do that with the following exercises.

*Exercise #1.* We know that John 2:5 narrates a conversation between Mary, Jesus, and two or more unnamed servants at a wedding feast in someone's home. Apparently Mary was speaking in the imperative, for Jesus had resisted her suggestions (*hypothesis*). John refers to this incident as the first miracle of Jesus (*analysis*). We can conclude from this that John did not record the event to prove that Mary exerted matriarchal authority. This event is recorded so that we may know the first miracle of Jesus. By logical extension, then, we can presume that this passage deals with the lordship of Jesus. We deduce that the details of the miraculous transformation of water into wine are less important than the fact that Jesus gave evidence of his lordship in many ways, one of which was performing miracles.

With these facts in mind, do the following experiment:

▼ Say aloud "and Mary said" without emphasis.

▼ Next, speak the quote evenly, but with little or no emphasis: "Whatsoever he says to do / you do it!"

▼ Then, experiment with varying degrees of emphasis: "*Whatsoever he says to do* / YOU DO IT."

The best oral interpretation lies somewhere between these examples. You should strive to develop the artistic use of vocal and physical expression that will convey the reader's suggested interpretation to the listeners (*application*). Your ability in this area will grow with experience.

*Exercise #2.* Psalm 73 offers changes of pace and changes of mood. This psalm is an oral interpreter's dream. Read this psalm three times from your favorite version, and then read it aloud following the suggestions indicated below. Use your best oral interpretation techniques. Picture in your mind someone asking, "Why do good people suffer?" Then, picture yourself as offering Psalm 73 (NIV) as an answer.

*(A pleasant beginning, anticipating agreement from those who listen.)*

1. Surely God is good to Israel, to those who are pure in heart.

*(A sudden change of mood, from positive to negative.)*

2. But as for me, my feet had almost slipped; I had nearly lost my foothold.

3. For I envied the arrogant when I saw the prosperity of the wicked.

*(The anger is now in full force.)*

4. They have no struggles; their bodies are healthy and strong.

5. They are free from the burdens common to man; they are not plagued by human ills.

6. Therefore pride is their necklace; they clothe themselves with violence.

7. From their callous hearts comes iniquity; the evil conceits of their minds know no limits.

8. They scoff, and speak with malice; in their arrogance they threaten oppression.

9. Their mouths lay claim to heaven, and their tongues take possession of the earth.

10. Therefore their people turn to them and drink up waters in abundance.

11. They say, "How can God know? Does the Most High have knowledge?"

*(The anger continues, but there is a transition sentence.)*

12. This is what the wicked are like—always carefree, they increase in wealth.

*(Forceful anger expressed again.)*

13. Surely in vain have I kept my heart pure; in vain have I washed my hands in innocence.

14. All day long I have been plagued; I have been punished every morning.

*(Anger begins to give way to reason.)*

15. If I had said, "I will speak thus," I would have betrayed your children.

16. When I tried to understand all this, it was oppressive to me

*(A major transition; a great turning point.)*

17. till I entered the sanctuary of God; then I understood their final destiny.

*(The awesome feeling of discerning the answer to a deeply perplexing question.)*

18. Surely you place them on slippery ground; you cast them down to ruin.

19. How suddenly are they destroyed, completely swept away by terrors!

20. As a dream when one awakes, so when you arise, O Lord, you will despise them as fantasies.

*(A transition, expressed in penitence.)*

21. When my heart was grieved and my spirit embittered,

22. I was senseless and ignorant; I was a brute beast before you.

*(A return to positive statements, possibly expressed exuberantly. Set to music, these verses might be a crescendo.)*

23. Yet I am always with you; you hold me by my right hand.

24. You guide me with your counsel, and afterward you will take me into glory.

25. Whom have I in heaven but you? And earth has nothing I desire besides you.

26. My flesh and my heart may fail, but God is the strength of my heart and my portion forever.

27. Those who are far from you will perish; you destroy all who are unfaithful to you.

28. But as for me, it is good to be near God. I have made the Sovereign LORD my refuge; I will tell of all your deeds.

▼

Sarrett, Foster, and Sarrett summarize the oral interpretation task as follows: "Writing, like notes in music, is just black marks on paper. But, like notes in music, it represents ideas, feelings, meanings that lived in the mind of the author or composer. The oral reader's job is to bring those black marks back to life in his own mind and body. Then, much as the violinist turns a musical score back into music, the reader uses his own mind, voice, and body as the instrument for making language come back to life for his listeners."[4]

This should be especially true in the public reading of Scripture. Many preachers staunchly defend the veracity of the Bible but read it aloud as though they had rarely seen it. Many preachers have the congregation stand "in respect for the reading of God's Holy Word." Standing may be one way to demonstrate respect for God's Word. But standing or sitting, the congregation should never hear Scripture read monotonously, offhandedly, or laboriously, as if it were a task to be endured before the sermonic "main event."

*The public reading of Scripture should be a highlight in the worship service.* Good oral interpretation magnifies the Word of God without calling attention to itself. A preacher or any reader of the Bible should be satisfied with no less than an inspiring, uplifting reading that can become "the very voice of God to their souls."

## Public Proclamation

Orally interpreting one's own sermon is a little less complicated than public Bible reading. The preparations for orally interpreting one's own sermon are as follows:

1. Practice preach your next sermon. Experiment with the vocal variables and body language until you find the best way to suggest the purpose or meaning of the message. Avoid being loud for the sake of being loud. Save the major emphases for those portions of the message that require it. Vary the rate so that relatively unimportant sections move a little more quickly than major assertions and conclusions. (Explanations and applications usually are spoken more slowly than illustrations.) Use pitch inflections to indicate transitions and to assist in making emphases. Use pauses to give the listener time to absorb information, or to set the stage for a major emphasis.

The first sentence of a sermon, for instance, should always be spoken conversationally, unless there is some reason to shout it or whisper it. The first sentence may be mundane: "The text for today is . . . ." Or, it may involve the congregation in some way: "You may have experienced the joy of leading someone to Christ . . . ." Or the first sentence could lead into an illustration: "You will recall that it was in 1973 that American prisoners of war were finally released from North Vietnam." It would be ludicrous to shout or whisper any of these opening sentences. In each case, content calls for a conversational tone. The proclaimer should always let content dictate how the message will be orally interpreted to the listeners.

2. Use a tape recorder, if possible a video recorder, to evaluate the delivery of your recent messages and to improve your delivery of future messages. Again, the best technique for evaluation and self-improvement is to transcribe a message (or portion of it) from the tape recorder just as it was preached. Remember, you will experience an initial shock when you see in writing what you said. (A strong side benefit of transcribing messages is that the intellectual message will be presented more clearly in future preaching opportunities.)

A videotape recording of the sermon has an obvious advantage. The videotape permits an analysis of both the vocal variables and body language. Listen carefully to see if you communicated important sections with emphasis, and if you deemphasized relatively unimportant sections. Listen for inflections and pauses that communicate transition from one thought to another. Listen for monotones, vocal patterns, and distracting habits such as lip smacking, vocalized pauses, or lazy speech.

Next, look to see if eye contact was strong, especially during key assertions. See if the body language supported and helped communicate the content. Watch for any distracting mannerisms such as body sway, rhythmic gestures, and annoying habits such as constantly pushing glasses up on the nose or licking the lips. These evaluation sessions will gradually dissolve hindrances to good speaking and enhance effective communication techniques.

These evaluation sessions should take place only before and after speaking opportunities—never during them. If they are done during a presentation, the speaker will be preoccupied. The delivery and the attention of the audience will be removed from the message. All of us make minor adjustments as we speak, but thorough evaluations should not take place during the proclamation.

3. Listen to and watch other preachers, especially those on television. Apply all of the criteria used in evaluating your-

self. See if you can determine whether the sermon delivery supports sermon content. If delivery does support content, listen to how the vocal variables are used, and watch how body language is used. If delivery does not support context, is it because of: a pitch pattern, misplaced vocal emphasis, narrow range of pitch/volume, a rate that is too rapid or too slow, lack of pauses, too many long pauses, distracting body language, lack of eye contact? Do you find yourself more attracted to the messenger or to the message? At the end of the sermon, could you imitate the preacher's sermon delivery? At the end of the sermon, could you say in one sentence of eighteen words or less how the sermon's biblical text applies to you? Could you give a three-minute synopsis of the sermon?

4. Use an evaluation form. At the end of this chapter is a sample of a comprehensive one. You may copy it, adapt it, or create your own.

## Image-Level Communication

The various speech techniques are not designed to call attention to themselves. If a congregation admires a speaker's voice or speech techniques, or if the congregation holds the communication process itself above the message being proclaimed, then the speaker has failed. The speech techniques in this book should lead to *image-level communication*. That is, listeners should see in their mind's eye what the speaker is saying. Each word, phrase, sentence, and paragraph should support the content so well that the congregation can picture what is being said. (Abstract ideas should be made concrete for the congregation.) Image-level communication means that the congregation will be looking at the speaker only through the speaker's message. (Many preachers pray, "Lord, hide me behind thy cross as I preach!" This book is an attempt to put hands, feet, body, and voice into that prayer.)

Image-level communication allows the congregation to see what is being said and also to feel it, to empathize with it. When the preacher establishes empathy, the listener is much more likely to respond to the speaker's invitation to take some specific action or to change an attitude. With image-level communication, commitments, and attitude changes are much more likely to be permanent than if the speaker depends on special gimmicks, or personal charm.

Careful preparation is necessary to maximize the message and minimize the messenger. Full vocal production gives the speaker the means of realizing the full potential of individual voice quality, and it preserves and protects the speaker's voice for service in the later years of life. Clear enunciation and articulation put a congregation at ease so they can listen to the message without trying to figure out what the speaker has said. Vocal variables give meaning to the message. Body language reinforces the message, and at times it even communicates in place of language. Oral interpretation integrates all of these speech functions in a way that makes the listener come alive to the Bible.

In preaching, as in most forms of Christian oral communication, we must remember that delivery is the servant of content. Both the message and the messenger are vital to preaching. Take one or the other away, and preaching cannot exist. But sermon content is always more important than sermon delivery. The messenger is never as important as the message. Ineffective delivery focuses attention on itself. Effective delivery, however, points beyond itself by supporting the message we have been commissioned to proclaim.

▼

# Sermon Evaluation Form

Name _____

Date _____

I. Elements of strength (Continue to work on these.
   What helped you?)

1. _____
2. _____
3. _____
4. _____
5. _____
6. _____

II. Elements for improvement (Work hard on these.
    What hindered you?)

1. _____
2. _____
3. _____
4. _____
5. _____
6. _____

III. Observe these during delivery. Mark "X" for "needs
     improvement" and "OK" for "satisfactory."

Sermon Content ( introduction, body, conclusion)

__ First sentence          ___ Text analysis
__ Reading of text         ___ Hermeneutics
__ Relates to people       ___ Objectives achieved
__ Title                   ___ Body points
__ Conclusion              ___ Explanation
__ Application             ___ Illustrations
__ Grammar                 ___ Humor

Sermon Delivery (oral, non-oral communication):

| | |
|---|---|
| __ Voice quality | __ Enunciation |
| __ Articulation | __ Pronunciation |
| __ Rate of Speech | __ Pitch |
| __ Volume | __ Phrasing |
| __ Energy/Vigor/Force | __ Use of notes, eye contact |
| __ Facial expression | __ Gestures/use of hands |
| __ Posture/body use | __ Personal appearance |

IV. Observe the following and enter the number that best applies: 1) superior, 2) above average, 3) average, 4) below average, or 5) poor.

__ Clarity (logical progression; use of words)
__ Beauty, appeal, human interest
__ Forcefulness
__ Biblical authority (relationship of sermon to text content)

V. Total Interest Level:

| Introduction | Body | Conclusion |
|---|---|---|

Mark "ups and downs" as you experience the message. (see the example below)

▼

# S I X

*We take radio and television for granted now, but [in 1926] radio was new, and its use for religious purposes was in an experimental stage . . . I had no idea of the possibilities involved. Frankly skeptical of its effect, I undertook it rather listlessly. I used to go down to the studio on Sunday afternoon and, sitting at a table, talk into that strange contrivance, the microphone, with no vivid sense of contact with the unseen audience. Later the microphone became to me almost as stirring as a great congregation, no longer a thing, but an almost living symbol of multitudes of individual people.*

Harry Emerson Fosdick
*The Living of These Days*

▼

# Delivery for Radio and Television

On Christmas Eve, 1906, Reginald Aubry Fessenden, a Canadian who loved to experiment, broadcast the world's first radio "program."[1] The program consisted of a poem, an aria from Handel's Messiah, a violin interpretation of "O Holy Night," Fessenden's reading of Luke 2:1–20, and a brief speech, probably a devotional. Days later, Fessenden's audience, made up of radio operators on ships at sea, shared with him the dramatic impact his program had made. They were astonished. After the steady drone of Morse code, they were more than startled to hear a human voice in their earphones. Some shared with their crew mates that they had thought the Second Coming had occurred. Most were accused of being drunk or crazy or both. The idea of transmitting a program over the air waves was a shock—a happy shock, but still a shock.

Broadcast historians usually cite the broadcast of presidential election returns of 1920 on KDKA in Pittsburgh, Pennsylvania, as the first radio program by a commercial station. At this time, what little evidence that exists suggests that Fessenden's 1906 Christmas Eve broadcast was history's first broadcast program. "Now you know the rest of the story": the first broadcast program had a specifically Christian message.

For a few years, the general public thought of the air waves as belonging to God. Care was taken to maintain dignity and decorum in radio programming. Commercials were considered this-worldly and materialistic. Many commercials were simply courtesy announcements, such as "The following program is brought to you by the Bell Telephone Company." Anything more was thought to be in bad taste.

Preachers were slow to catch on to the power of radio. The huge microphones near the pulpit seemed intrusive. Besides, God's Word had been proclaimed without radio for centuries. Translated, that meant, "We have never done it this way before." The networks, primarily NBC, encouraged preachers to think in terms of radio. Letters from listeners soon convinced preachers that radio could stretch their ministries far beyond the church walls. Suddenly, preachers vied for air time and even obtained licenses for church-owned radio stations.

In the 1920s, sixty-three churches were licensed to operate radio stations, but this number soon declined. Then, as now, a broadcast operation was expensive, and most churches let their licenses lapse during the Great Depression of the 1930s. By the end of World War II, most of these licenses had been claimed by other businesses.

Many commercial stations of that decade were network affiliated. The networks, especially NBC, encouraged religious and other public-service programming and required their affiliate stations to carry these programs free of charge. Consequently, local radio stations had no free time to give for local church programs. Stations charged churches to broadcast their worship services. This policy of assessing a fee for broadcast time for local churches still exists, though many stations charge less for churches than they do for other institutions. Television stations have adopted similar policies.

Station managers discovered, though, that requiring churches to pay for air time had an additional advantage. It was one way that local radio and television stations could screen church applicants for broadcast times. The local station was and is responsible for both the technical quality and the content of any program it puts on the air. Some stations had been embarrassed by the poor quality and content of religious programs. For that reason, local church leaders (or anyone else wishing to purchase air time for a religious program) had to convince officials of the station of their integrity and solvency. Station managers appreciate and love to work with churches that recognize the strictures of broadcast law and the audience's demand for high-quality programming.

Speaking on radio or television is different from speaking to a local congregation. Preachers do well to follow certain guidelines, even in broadcasting their Sunday morning services. These guidelines will help guarantee high-quality programming and good audience reception.

## Guidelines for Christian Programs on Radio

1. *Speak in a manner that is authoritative, urgent, and sincere.* Listeners develop impressions of the speaker only on the basis of the sound of the speaker's voice. The radio audience will picture the speaker in their minds. Their mental images rarely stand the test of reality. With few exceptions, when a listener meets the speaker, the listener will generally say, "You do not look at all like you sound." The speaker cannot control these mental images of physical appearance but can strive to convey a mental impression of the speaker as a congenial, dependable Christian. "Even without the assistance of visual cues, it is clear that a listener is responding not only to the message content but to the 'image of the speaker'."[2] P. D. Holtzman adds: "The listeners are not necessarily responding to the speaker as he actually exists. They are responding to the perceived speaker as he is comprehended and interpreted by the listeners' nervous systems."[3]

Speak in a manner that is authoritative, urgent, and sincere. The message should be *authoritative* because it is based on the Bible. The message should be *urgent* because the speaker has a message the listener needs right now. The message should be sincere because the speaker believes in the message and knows the listeners need to hear it for their own good. Listeners should sense this. In fact, they should feel that they would like to invite the speaker over to dinner.

That is a deep level of confidence and a lot to ask of a listener who has never met the speaker. However, that kind of confidence is necessary if the listener is to receive the speaker as a credible source.

2. *Respect your time limits.* Broadcasters are, by necessity, slaves of the clock. The station manager or program director usually will state the time limits for a local program. The perils of ignoring time limits in any broadcasting operation are serious. If a local church, for example, buys an hour of air time per week for 10:00 A.M. Sunday, and another church is scheduled for 11:00 A.M., the station is forced to observe the time limit closely. If the ten o'clock program lasts 60 minutes/15 seconds, the eleven o'clock church program will either be put on the air late if it is on tape, or it will be joined in progress. Either way, listeners generally will conclude, "Our local station messed up again." If the ten o'clock program lasts fifty-six minutes instead of fifty-nine minutes, the local station is put in an awkward situation of filling in the three-minute gap—perhaps by playing organ music or reading public service announcements.

3. *Strive for acceptable technical quality.* This is usually a problem for a church that has its own recording equipment. (Churches that record or broadcast their programs on station equipment usually will not have this concern.) Reliable and efficient broadcast equipment is expensive, and maintaining the equipment is also expensive. A local church considering the purchase of its own equipment should consult technicians in the field. It is mandatory to make budget provisions for both the initial purchase of its equipment and for its continual maintenance.

4. *Make sure that the content of your program does not cause difficulty for your local radio station.* A conference with the station manager will clarify Federal Communications Commission laws pertaining to the fairness doctrine. These laws have been relaxed in recent years but most station managers still prefer to be fair in their service to the entire community. They expect churches to understand their concerns for fairness. The old fairness doctrine demanded that licensed stations devote time to controversial issues, and they always afforded equal time for opposing view-

points. The fairness doctrine laws came into being in 1929.[4] As with many legal matters, challenges to this law cause constant adjustments and crystallization. As the law evolved, the local station had to justify its existence by serving the "public interest, convenience, or necessity" of the local community. Religious programming was considered to be in the public interest and convenience, but it was subject to the fairness doctrine. The church-related programs under the law could be completely devoted to preaching the gospel. But when the sermon or lesson involved controversial issues, such as abortion, race relations, or homosexuality, the local broadcaster was bound by law to give persons with opposing viewpoints the opportunity to express their side of the issue. In addition, the station was compelled to offer this response time free of charge.

Ideally, the content of the radio program should be basic information that meets some vital need.[5] Rare and perhaps nonexistent is the radio audience, for example, that is prepared to listen to a discussion about the history of the Kenites. The radio message should focus on some vital concern of the listeners, such as problems in the contemporary home.

5. *Appeal to human interest.* Human interest simply means referring to people whenever that is appropriate. To create human interest, simply mention people at every opportunity in your message. For example, the biblical text of the message usually will involve one or more persons. Jesus was a master at increasing the appeal of his messages with human interest: "A certain man had two sons. . . ." "A sower went out to sow. . . . " We could cite many other examples from the Bible. In fact, the Bible, to borrow a fitting rural phrase, is "chock full" of people. Every doctrine in the Bible relates itself to people. Acts 17:16–34, for instance, loses its impact if it is studied only as a lesson in congregational analysis; but this story comes alive when we see Paul and the ways different people responded to his message. Modern preachers can learn much from the Bible about the importance of the human element in communication. Human interest prevents a dry, abstract message that lacks image-level communication.

6. *Paint word-pictures.* Word-pictures are vital to a good radio program. They need not be elaborate, but they should be specific. Radio, used effectively, piques the imagination. Radio preachers must think in terms of painting specific word-pictures. Think, for example, of how many synonyms are available for the verb *walk*, and how each conveys a different picture.

▼ The lady walked into the store. (Image-level communication is weak.)

▼ The lady shuffled into the store. (A specific picture!)

▼ The lady strutted into the store. (An entirely different picture!)

A thesaurus is invaluable to the radio speaker in developing a vocabulary that will improve image-level communication.

7. *Avoid clichés and preacher talk.* These convey the image of a professional religionist interested only in shallow answers rather than a warm person with an urgent and vital message. Here are some clichés from sermons I have heard:

### Preacher Talk

▼ "Turn over in your Bibles . . ." (someone may take that literally).

▼ "Turn with me, if you would . . ." ("if you would" may be courteous, but it is overworked).

▼ "Beloved" or "brethren" (never used in conversation except by preachers).

### Hyberbole

▼ "This is the most tragic story you will ever hear . . ." (until next Sunday, when I must come up with another tear-jerker).

▼ "The temple was completely destroyed, completely demolished, completely ravaged, completely ruined . . ." (and every redundancy diminishes the strength of the word "completely").

### Doublespeak[6]

▼ "a few short miles to church . . ." (are these miles less than 5,280 feet?).

▼ "a few short minutes . . ." (again, do some minutes contain less than sixty seconds?).

### Overstating the Obvious

▼ "The President was assassinated two days ago. As he was being driven through a downtown street, waving to the cheering crowd, shots rang out. . . ." (Who in the congregation would not know the details two days later?)

▼ "The flood was caused by an excess of water on the ground." (This is quoted from an unpublished sermon on Noah.)

### Specialized Theological Wording

▼ "Are you responding to the promise of the coming eschaton?" (This question was asked of a new convert!)

▼ "What is your view of docetism?" (Someone asked this of a new convert!)

### Abuse of Technical Language

▼ "If you could read Greek and Hebrew, you could understand what I am preaching." (Greek and Hebrew should be tools the preacher uses to help people understand.)

▼ "Obviously Peter is using an anacoluthon. . . ." (Impressive sounding, but way above the heads of the congregation.)

### Misleading Word Order

▼ "Let me illustrate: With a broken tail bone and a fractured skull, I shall never forget the auto accident. . . ." (No, the preacher meant someone else had a broken tail bone and fractured skull, not himself.)

▼ "For sale. Small chairs for children with straw seats." (Featured in an advertisement from a church.)

### Clichés

▼ "There is good and bad in all of us."

▼ "All things must come to an end."

## The Challenges of Television Programming

Television broadcasting has much more immediate impact and much more prestige connected with it than radio broadcasting has. This is because the audience can make a visual as well as audio evaluation of the speaker and because people spend more time watching television than listening to radio. Most people watch television about twenty to thirty hours weekly. How can we measure the effect of this much television viewing on the individual and collective psyches? In fact, we are only now learning which questions to ask in measuring the influence of television on the way a person thinks. The opening salvoes in this field of study have been pointedly stated and somewhat predictable.

John R. W. Stott sees at least five negative influences: (1) physical laziness, (2) intellectual passiveness, (3) emotional insensitivity, (4) psychological confusion, and (5) moral disorder.[7] Stott asks, "How easily can people switch from one world [television] to the other? Do they recognize, when they hear God's word and worship him, that now at least they are in touch with eternal reality? Or do they, as I fear, move from one unreal situation to another, somnambulating as in a dream because television has introduced them to a world of fantasy from which they never escape?"[8]

The same moral question has also been raised by Martin E. Marty:

> The media . . . set out to shape in men 'the proper opinions,' to make them common men and women, unknown citizens somehow at the mercy of the communicator. Because of the hours of attention they command and the apparent quality that is theirs owing to the economic potential, they usually achieve this aim. It is in such a world that Christianity makes its claim and its offer. It presents a paradox, a foolishness, something 'contrary to the opinion.' It has an improper opinion for the common man; for the known citizen of the commonwealth whose builder and maker is God.[9]

Harold J. Ellens quoted this excerpt from Marty's book, and expressed the same concern: "The mass media has become potent arbiters of value in our society, and the cultural and spiritual idealism they communicate will eventually shape our culture and society. In the final analysis, humans become in large part what they are taught to digest and/or confess."[10]

Quentin Schultze, who has written several significant books related to Christianity and television, made these incisive, highly practical comments:

Nothing has kept Christians and others from redeeming television more than the misguided belief that every program must teach or instruct people about the gospel of Jesus Christ. In evangelical circles, the narrow linking of the tube with the Great Commission has resulted ironically in few programs that actually reach nonbelievers. Television, as a narrative medium, can be used effectively to amuse, instruct, confirm and illuminate. Whatever stories can do, television can also do—and surely it is the most popular storyteller of our age. If television is truly going to be used to spread the good news, Christian producers must be creative storytellers through drama and documentary, not just Bible teachers or talk-show hosts. In short, believers must seize the medium for the breadth of its cultural potential, not just for is apparent power to propagandize.[11]

The local church or individual Christian who aspires to communicate a Christian message on television must be aware of these ethical imperatives in program production. The person who would preach on television must concentrate on presenting a positive gospel message that relates to the needs of the contemporary audience.

The Christian broadcaster must ardently avoid building a cult of personality. This is a great temptation for many persons who appear on television. Essentially, the temptation seems to take this line of rationalization: "If you really matter, you will be at the focus of mass attention, and if you are the focus of mass attention, then surely you must really matter."[12] The use of television increases the temptation to maximize the messenger rather than the message. That means the messenger receives the recognition and glory that should go to God; the messenger speaks only for self-promotion and self-gain. (This is nothing new. Acts 19:13–16 records how two men tried to exploit the name of Jesus and paid an embarrassing price for their efforts! Perhaps, the same thing should happen to today's sons of Sceva.) All Christian workers, especially those in broadcasting, would do well to study Acts 12:22–24 and Acts 14:11–15. In Christian broadcasting, therefore, the imperative to magnify the message and minimize the messenger is critically important.

## Guidelines for Christian Programs on Television

The technical suggestions for producing a Christian television program are similar to some of those outlined for radio. As on radio, you should remember that the station is a slave to the clock; use the facilities of a local television station or be certain that your program is recorded on high-quality equipment that is regularly maintained; and be certain that the content is appealing and does not cause unnecessary difficulty for the local station. Several considerations should be added, however.

1. *Create visual variety.* Television is a visual medium. This seems obvious enough, but many persons treat television merely as an audio medium in which the audience sees the speaker. The most boring picture on television is the "talking head." (A talking head is a picture of the speaker looking at the camera with the lens zoomed in so that the viewer sees only the shoulders, neck, and face of the speaker.) Plan to give variety by using slides, films, and photographs that picture the content of the message. The visual stimulation will help the audience immensely. Observe how various television programs and commercials use not only the actors, but other visual stimuli. Notice how briefly each picture or camera angle stays on the screen before it is changed. (This "flitting" of pictures may not be good for the Christian program because it limits rather than focuses the attention span of the viewer.) Using visuals requires lots of time in planning, editing, and rehearsing. The entire process is expensive. These production decisions need to be thought through and evaluated by the local church if the church is to make maximum use of television as a visual medium.

2. *Be aware of your on-camera stage presence.* Stage presence communicates either a sense of rapport and self-confidence or a lack of it. Notice the contrasts, for instance, in a "game show" that calls for members of the audience to appear on stage. The host always seems to look "just right," but the audience participant betrays a sense of awkwardness in posture, facial expressions, and vocal variables. The host, who has many years of experience, will act with authority and confidence. This is due in large part to innate talent, but it is also due to instruction and experience. (Most of us develop a sense of relaxation, self-confidence, and authority as we gain experience in any endeavor. This is especially true in broadcasting.)

The professional uses good posture (never rigid or slouched). The professional will have a low eye-blink rate (the frequency of eye blinking conveys a feeling of insecurity). The professional uses only necessary gestures. All this is in strong contrast to those who are inexperienced.

The general physical appearance of the professional appears to be good, usually full of vitality and trim in physique.

The amateur in broadcasting can acquire these professional qualities (including a sense of vitality and a trim physique). Chapters 1–3 of this book are basic to achieving the "professional" look on television with one exception: television gestures must be slow and deliberate, never made directly toward the camera.

3. *Communicate a sense of confidence.* When the floor director calls for you to take your place on the set, do not be intimidated by the situation. Look upon this moment as an opportunity to speak to people about Christ. The floor director will position you at a slight angle to the camera. You will need to keep your head high (as opposed to resting on your chest), and place your body weight on the front foot. To do so will avoid a sense of withdrawal and intimidation. As noted before, the audience will be more attracted to a clear message from a person who communicates a sense of urgency and sincerity rather than from one who creates a sense of uncertainty and timidity.

4. *Maintain strong eye contact with your congregation.* Plan to have "eye" contact at least 90 percent of the time. When not looking at your congregation, look only at your Bible and notes. Avoid looking at the ceiling or at any place where there are no people.

5. *Avoid looking at the monitor while on camera.* Do not glance at the monitor to see how you look on television. (For certain, do not make cosmetic adjustments, such as straightening your eye brows, while on camera.)

6. *Do not be disappointed if the local television station does not have a chapel from which religion programs are telecast.* When the worship service is broadcast from or taped at a television studio, you will need to use whatever props the station may have. The set for a program is never as attractive in the studio as it appears on screen. The "chapel" will be made of cardboard backdrops located in a corner of a massive studio, and the bare concrete floor will be covered with heavy electrical wires. A forest of lights will droop from the ceiling, and they will be bright and warm. The speaker will want to become acclimated to the brightness and heat of these lights before the program begins.

7. *Advise people who are part of your program not to ask the director if they can be featured on camera sometime during the program.* Choir members, for instance, who are afraid they will be lost in a sea of faces often make this request. Television production crew personnel say that these requests, which are numerous, generally begin this way: "Sir, I would not ask this for myself, but I have a sick grandmother and it would make her feel ever so good if you would direct the camera on me during the choir number. You understand it doesn't make any difference to me. . . ." The production crew often wonders whether anyone does a Christian program only for the glory of God.

8. *Maintain a vivacious, energetic level throughout the program.* Leave the audience feeling that you have more to say and plenty of energy with which to say it, and that you simply have run out of time. This will help the audience look forward to your next program. The speaker who ends the program with a gravelly voice, beleaguered expression,

slouching posture, coat off, tie loose, top button of shirt unbuttoned, soaked with sweat, and standing on six inches of his trousers leg may leave the audience feeling they have seen and heard all that this man has to offer, and next week will be merely a repeat. (In fact, this is one of the dangers of the cult of personality in religious programming. The audience should be looking forward to hearing the message, not to viewing the performance of the messenger.)

9. *Strive to attain the highest technical quality.* Appeal to a large audience, urgently share the message of Christ, and use the powerful influence of television in the best possible ways.

10. *Magnify the message rather than the messenger.* Television should never be used for personal aggrandizement. This cannot be emphasized too much for the Christian broadcaster. The first television preacher to receive wide acclaim was Bishop Fulton J. Sheen. He avoided building a cult of personality by applying this strong biblical dictum:

> On television, he who appears before the public may well ask himself: "What powers hast thou, that did not come to thee by gift? And if they came to thee by gift, why dost thou boast of them as if there were no gift in question? . . . No praise therefore is due the author of these telecasts. If there be gratitude for putting them into print, the author accepts it as the window receives light; namely, to pass thanks back again to God, the author of all good gifts. However, the imperfections, the failings, and the marring of the gifts are due to the window itself.[13]

Christians involved in radio and television programming should ardently avoid the temptation to build personal empires. This is done, as always, by magnifying the message and minimizing the messenger.

Many directors and production managers at television stations will be happy to help the Christian programmer. These technicians can share valuable advice about how to use television equipment. They also will expose you to published information about writing and producing effective programs.

▼

# S E V E N

"*I shall not detain you any longer, but express the hope that your chest, lungs, windpipe, larynx, and all your vocal organs may last till you have nothing more to say.*"

Charles Haddon Spurgeon
*Lectures to My Students*

# Ten Frequent Questions about Sermon Delivery

This book began as a series of lectures to seminary preaching classes and other preaching conferences. This chapter includes the ten questions that preachers have most often asked in those groups. Here are the ten questions in order of frequency, each followed by my response.

## Question #1

When I prepare my sermons, I think in a formal writing style. When I preach my sermons, my writing style sounds forced and stilted. How can I write my sermons in a way that will sound smooth when I preach them?

———

Most of us are burdened with this problem. We are required—wisely, I think—to take courses in English where, among other things, we learn to express ourselves through writing. Few of us were required to take courses in speech, where we are taught to express ourselves orally. (I admire those people whose writing style and speaking style are virtually the same.)

So, how do we develop an oral style in our sermon preparation? My early training as a broadcast journalist helps me answer this question. When we covered a news event, we were taught to see and to listen for details. When we wrote our stories, we were told to describe orally what we saw and

———

heard. (Usually we did this with the assistance of notes and audio-video tapes.) In the description we were taught to begin with the most important details, work our way down through the less important, and conclude with incidental details. At first I had to record my oral descriptions on an audio cassette. This was usually done on the way back to the station. At the station I would type the story from my tape. In the beginning, I had to do some editing of my oral description. In a short time, though, I learned to determine which details were important and how I would describe them on the air. Throughout the process, I was asking myself, "How will I say what I am seeing and hearing?" Not "How will I write?" but "How will I say my description to my audience?"

For instance, if I were assigned to report on a traffic accident, my list of details would look something like this:

4 people hurt
Driver (male) of car—serious injuries; taken to local hospital
Passenger treated at scene—minor injuries; driver of truck—not hurt
Passenger in truck—minor scratches and bruises
Police officer said—collision head on—cause of accident unknown
Skid marks indicate both vehicles exceeded speed limit
Car—4-door
Truck—pickup, no load
No other witnesses
Time of accident—2:05 P.M.
Location: intersection of 10th and Vine—no traffic light
Traffic blocked both directions
Two police cars, one ambulance, two tow trucks
Rear wheels of car on curb
Car and truck both GM

From this list I could easily make an oral description:

Four people were injured, one seriously, this afternoon when a car and truck collided head-on near Tenth and Vine. The injured man was taken by ambulance to the local hospital. Police on the scene said both vehicles were apparently exceeding the speed limit. They are not certain at this time why the accident occurred.

This process works well in sermon preparation. Make a careful study of the biblical text. Find the important details and list them first. Then find the secondary or marginal ideas and list them last. From your list, state the main idea of the text in a brief, declarative sentence of eighteen words or less. Do the same thinking with your secondary and marginal ideas. Occasionally, your sermons will come from these other ideas in the text. For more information about preaching the central idea or other ideas of a text, see *Steps to the Sermon* by Brown, Clinard, Northcutt, and Fasol (rev. ed., Nashville: Broadman & Holman, 1996).

Write the central idea (or secondary idea, or marginal idea) at the top of a sheet of paper. Begin by talking about this idea into a tape recorder. From your tape, jot down some key words, phrases, or sentences. These key words become the "pegs" upon which you hang your oral thoughts. Talk through your sermon in this manner two or three times. You will be amazed at how much information you can retain in preparation for preaching. If necessary, write a sermon from your taped descriptions. Stay with your oral style as you write.

This process is different for each of us. I preach without notes almost all the time. Key words in the text are my "pegs." As I study my text, I develop a mental image of what the text says. This is very important because I am thinking in terms of concrete images rather than abstract precepts. I describe to the congregation what I "see" in my mind. They, in turn, "see" the images I am trying to convey. This image-level process is a strong way to communicate, and is absolutely necessary in preaching.

## Question #2

I have abused my voice. I've tried the exercises you suggest and they have helped a lot. But I feel uncertain if I am using full vocal production or not. I am a novice. How can I be sure I am using full vocal production?

—

In at least two ways. The most obvious way for you to know if you are using full vocal production is by how your vocal cords feel. Are you feeling any soreness or strain during and after your sermons? I remember when you first came to me last year. You said you had a "tired" throat on Sunday afternoon and dreaded preaching on Sunday night. You said you had "laryngitis" on Mondays at first, and the condition began to persist until Tuesday, and then till Wednesday. That was when you came to me. Now that you no longer have laryngitis on Monday, or even a "tired" throat on Sunday afternoon, you are doing something right. Since you are not feeling any strain in your throat, I think you can be sure that you are using full vocal production. Just remember how tense and dry and strained your throat felt when you preached before you did these exercises. Compare that to how relaxed and free you feel when you preach these days. Your first, and maybe most important, assurance that you are using full vocal production is the lack of strain on your vocal cords as you preach.

The second way for you to know if you are using full vocal production is how your voice sounds. You may find it a little difficult to determine if you sound differently. Perhaps other persons—for example, your spouse—could tell if your voice sounds clear and strong. When you are not using full vocal production, your voice will usually have a higher pitch, your voice will sound dry and gravelly (especially toward the end of the sermon). You will find yourself limited in making inflections and in using volume to make emphases, and you will find yourself retreating to a dramatic whisper in order not to tax your voice any longer. (You may occasionally use a dramatic whisper to support content, but you should never need to use the dramatic whisper to protect your voice. Instead, develop your full vocal production and use your voice effectively all the time.) You can usually feel, as well as hear, when your voice is clear and resonant instead of gravelly and strained.

Remember, you must do your full vocal production exercises several times a week; better yet, do them daily. Full vocal production depends on many different muscles. When these muscles are in good condition, your voice will be strong, clear, and resonant. Review chapter 1 for these exercises. Develop your own exercises.

In this discipline, we can identify with Paul: We have not yet attained, we reach forth unto those things which are before, pressing toward the mark (Phil. 3:12–14).

## Question #3

My question is related to the previous one. I have been following your voice exercise program since my first sermon. My wife says the exercises have really helped me. She says I should be able to preach with a clear voice when I am ninety years old. And I believe her until allergy season arrives. How do I protect my voice when sinus drainage has given me a sore throat? Can full vocal production help me when I am really sick? I mean by "sick," that my throat is sore not because I have abused my voice but because of my allergies.

———

By all means, full vocal production will help you when you must preach despite a sore throat. Still it would be far better if you did not speak at all during those times. I know that many of you do not have that option—or at least feel you do not have that option. If you must preach even though you have a sore throat, I have a few suggestions. I also have a few suggestions about preventing sore throats. (I wish I had a cure for allergies and sore throats. I would patent it and get rich quick!)

First, however, I must say that I am not trained as a physician. What I share with you now are observations from my own experiences with allergies and sore throats. Like Paul, I have a beloved physician (his name is David, not Luke) and I take my throat problems to him. However, when I awake on a Sunday morning with a sore throat, and neither David nor a substitute preacher is available, here are my guidelines for easing the situation.

1. Determine how loudly you can speak without pain, and speak no more loudly than that. Perhaps the microphone volume will need to be increased drastically. So be it. Better to have a little distortion in sound and less strain on your vocal cords. Perhaps there is no microphone and some people will be unable to hear very well. So be it.

Better they move toward the front for one or two services than for you to cause additional damage to your vocal cords. Perhaps you will have to stop and drink some water, or speak with a lozenge in your mouth, or just stop long enough to relax your voice. So be it. Better to have some awkward pauses than to keep on preaching until you cannot speak at all.

2. Do not open your sermon with an apology for the condition of your voice. For one thing, you need to speak as few words as possible. For another, your listeners will be sympathetic and prayerful as soon as they hear you speak. This is an occasion for using words carefully. (Actually, that should be true if we have a sore throat or not!) Do not waste your voice or the congregation's time with an apology. Abbreviate your sermon. Preach only what is essential. Stop preaching after ten or fifteen minutes (most congregations will appreciate that; in fact, they will consider you wise for not prolonging your agony).

3. Take medication only on a physician's advice. Once I used a throat spray. I read the label carefully. I understood from the label that the spray would alleviate my pain by numbing my throat. I could speak much more clearly for a short time after using the spray. But I also understood that I could do serious damage to my voice. If I projected my voice too strongly while my throat was numb, I could strain my voice and not even feel it. I used the spray, but I still spoke carefully and softly.

(On another occasion, a man handed me a lemon cut in two. He suggested I suck on the lemon during the song service. I did so—out of the view of everyone else—and it helped. I don't know why it helped, but it did.)

4. Do your best to avoid situations that cause you to have a sore throat. (The first thing I thought of when I heard that suggestion was to hold my breath until allergy season passed.) For myself, I noticed most of my sore throats occurred in January. Central heating dehumidifies air. Dryness in the nose and throat evidently made me more susceptible to throat problems. Since resolving that problem, I have had fewer throat problems.

One physician informed me that my throat problems were caused by stress. He may be correct, but I seem to have as many or as few problems with stress in other months of the year as I do in January. As I said, I am not trained in this area. I offer these suggestions from my own experience. You must rely on your own physician for answers to your individual problems.

## Question #4

Many preachers speak one way in the pulpit but another way everywhere else. Some preachers are more intense and loud. Others try to "deepen" their voices. I heard what you said about speech patterns and about the ministerial tone. But shouldn't the sermon sound different from the way we ordinarily speak? Also, does it hurt our voices if we speak differently when we preach?

———

I am disturbed when you say preachers speak differently in the pulpit. We must not become another person when we enter the pulpit. Think of it this way: God saw in you some particular quality or qualities he wanted and needed. Therefore, he called you to be a preacher. If we say we cannot be the person God called, but instead we must take on the persona of a "preacher" (whatever that is), it is the same as telling God he didn't know what he was doing when he called us. So, we offer to help God by correcting his "mistake." We decide we will not be the person God called, we will be someone else; we will be more like a "preacher." God forbid! Be true to yourself in the pulpit and everywhere else. Always try to grow in grace, to grow as a preacher, but do not take on a special pulpit identity. God saw something in you, and he called you forth. Determine to be the best you can be as a preacher and as a Christian.

Yet speaking in the pulpit *is* a different kind of speaking situation. Think of preaching this way. Suppose someone asks you a question—a question about Jesus. You are happy to give the best answer you can. You speak pleasantly, conversationally, and directly to the person. Next, suppose a few other people are interested in what you have to say. They stand next to and behind the person who asked the question. You enjoy telling about Jesus, so you do not see this as an intrusion. You are happy for them to hear your answer, too. You do make a little adjustment in your speaking. You project your voice a little so the persons standing behind can hear, and you expand your eye contact and your body language so the others will feel included. Take the process one more step. Many more people join the group. You make the same adjustments so all may hear your answer. During your answer you explain some things about Jesus; you might use an illustration or two, and you might apply the answer to the many people now listening. At what point did you cease being conversational and begin to "speak differently"?

Preaching may sound different because we must project our voices and expand our body language. But basically, we are just persons (called persons) sharing with some other persons. We are just being ourselves, but projecting ourselves a little so everyone can hear and feel the message we are called to preach.

You mentioned that some preachers try to "deepen" their voices. That is always a mistake. As we discussed (see chapter 1), we each have a distinctive vocal quality. We can and should strive to use our voices effectively, but it is a serious mistake to change our tone qualities superficially. The best way to "deepen" our voices is by using full vocal production. The resonance we achieve with full vocal production will provide all the vocal depth we need. Besides, doesn't it sound insincere when you hear someone deliberately changing his voice just for the sermon? We had a word for this in my youth—hoaky (sometimes spelled hokey). And let me add quickly, "deepening" the voice damages our vocal cords.

Let me speak to a related subject. Preachers are noted for their intense delivery style. Some preachers add ministerial tone to their intensity, but for right now let's just consider why so many preachers feel they must speak with an intensity that they might not use on other speaking occasions.

First, the message we proclaim is an urgent one. This is especially true when we preach an evangelistic message. The very urgency of our message heightens the intensity in our delivery.

Second, various communication studies indicate higher levels of intensity are more quickly persuasive than lower levels of intensity. These studies were done primarily with political speeches and sales pitches, but I think the principle holds true for preaching as well. Still, be yourself in the pulpit. If your gift is in high intensity preaching, be true to your gift. If your gift is in a more moderate level of intensity, be true to your gift. God has a place of service for all of us.

## Question #5

We have talked about delivery as it relates to "regular" sermons. What about when I preach narratives, or dramatic monologues, or sermons on a biblical character? Should I change my delivery for these sermons? I don't mean should I be something other than who I am. I mean are there special delivery techniques for special sermons?

—

The only techniques you need are found in your use of vocal variables (see chapter 3). The more agile you are with vocal variables, the more easily you will be able to adapt yourself to these other sermon forms. In every case, the adjustments are minor, but they are also necessary.

For the narrative sermon, you are conveying a setting, the characters, the plot, and the purpose or moral of the story. To do this, you will need a wide range of inflections, a general slowing down in rate, and effective use of facial expressions to help the congregation "feel" the story.

The congregation is more dependent on you during the narrative sermon. They depend on you to give them signals that alert them to the mood and cadence of the narrative. Without strong inflections, the congregation will be uncertain about what it is you are trying to say. Strong inflections demand a slower rate—we cannot rush a strong inflection. Facial expressions reinforce what our voices are conveying. Facial expressions also help, though nonverbally, during our pauses. Like background music in a movie, facial expressions set the tone or moral of the story.

The same things could be said of dramatic monologues. But with dramatic monologue, we must also talk about our use of body movements. If you are portraying only one person in your dramatic monologue, you will want to change positions on the platform from time to time. Suppose you are portraying the apostle Thomas when he hears Jesus say he would go to Bethany. As "Thomas," you would raise your eyebrows in disbelief, then step to another part of the platform as if separating yourself from the rest of the disciples, then return to the group and say, "Let us go, that we may die with him" (John 11:16). These movements are important to the congregation because they convey the emotion or pathos of the moment.

Let me say something about multimedia sermons. The preacher will use the same techniques called for in the narrative sermon. The main difference is that rate and pauses must be adjusted to coincide with the pictures or other sounds that are part of the presentation. Multimedia presentations are time-consuming and expensive because they usually include slides, recorded sounds, and/or other participants. Pictures must appropriately complement the sermon. Sounds—crowd noise, for example—must be recorded. Rehearsals are needed to iron out details of the presentation. Multimedia presentations can be immensely effective, but many preachers find the preparation too demanding.

A sermon on a biblical character requires the preacher to use vocal variables that support content. That is, the sermon on a biblical character may be preached in much the same way that any consecrative or doctrinal sermon may be preached. I am not trying to oversimplify. Every sermon, regardless of its form, presents a new challenge for the preacher. No two sermons can be preached in exactly the same way. The purpose of sermon delivery is to maximize the message and minimize the messenger. Since the content is different in every sermon, our delivery will always be a little different as well.

## Question #6

Does it help to listen to other preachers, and, if so, who are some preachers you would recommend?

We can always learn from others. When I first became interested in communications, I listened to as many people as I could. I listened to Douglas Edwards and later Walter Cronkite on the *CBS Evening News*. I listened to their inflections, their pauses, and their rate. They did not vary their volume very much—I guess that was because they were newscasters. I listened to the voices behind various commercials. The man who did the Kraft commercials—I believe his name was Ed Herlihy—had the smoothest voice and delivery I ever heard. I listened carefully and learned that his smoothness came from using inflections not only at the beginning of a word, but also *within* the word. I listened to various actors to determine why some were convincing in their portrayals and others were not. In every situation—from newscaster to actor—I learned how their use of vocal variables and their use of body language made the difference between a great communicator and an average communicator.

I also listened to preachers. Some preachers were strong and dynamic. Others were quieter, but they still communicated a sense of vitality. I noticed that preachers in non-evangelical churches were often subdued, even speaking in monotone. So, yes, it does help to listen to other preachers. It helps to listen to effective communicators wherever they may be found.

But there is a danger. When we listen to other speakers, we tend to imitate them. When we imitate other speakers, we almost always imitate their weaknesses rather than their strengths. And what is worse, when we imitate their strengths, we do such a poor job of it; and what is strength in speaking for others is simply another weakness in speaking for us. Even if we imitate another speaker's strength effectively, the congregation recognizes what we are doing and says, "Oh, look. He's imitating Billy Graham!"

Listen to other speakers, but resist the temptation to end up sounding like the last person you heard. Learn from others, but when it is time for you to preach, be yourself.

## Question #7

It seems to me that you are providing us the tools to manipulate and exploit people. With all these special techniques and ways of using our voices, won't we have the power to manipulate others? Isn't what you're teaching us really a means of exercising power over people?

---

What you say is *potentially* true. The skillful use of words, the effective use of voice and body certainly could be used to control or manipulate and perhaps even to exploit people. Historically, your concern can be well documented. The great Greek rhetoricians—Aristotle, for one—warned against self-ambition in their discourses on persuasion. The Jim Jones tragedy in Guiana shows us how a powerful speaker can exploit an audience.

Manipulation and exploitation are, however, not intrinsic to good sermon delivery. Manipulation and exploitation begin in the heart of the speaker rather than the voice of the speaker. If our desire is to manipulate and exploit, then yes, these tools of delivery can be used to do just that. If our motivation is to serve God, then these sermon delivery tools will be used to glorify him. Our motivations are the key here.

Despite our best intentions, some people may respond to us rather than respond to our message. Jesus' apostles met this problem; they had to prohibit people from worshiping them. When people respond to us rather than to the Christ we preach, we must set them straight.

The answer to your question is this: Keep your heart right with God and be the best preacher you can be.

## Question #8

You have shared so many things that rather than helping my preaching, I think you may have hindered it. I mean, how can I think about my sermon content, my breathing, the sound of my voice, my inflections, my pitch patterns, my volume, my rate, the length of my pauses, my gestures, my eye contact, my posture, my facial expressions, my oral interpretation—how can I be thinking of all of that and still preach?

---

You have a valid concern. No one could be thinking of all these things and still preach. In fact, you should not think of those things as you preach. Instead, think of—work on—those things as you *prepare* to preach. As you prepare your sermon, practice your sermon. Practice your sermon with a tape recorder. Listen to how delivery does or does not support content. Experiment with your volume, your pitch, your pause, your rate. Determine how you can make delivery support content. Do these things before you enter the pulpit, not while you are in the pulpit.

Do you play golf without any practice time, or without any warm-up? If you want to play effectively, you spend some time on the driving range, on the putting greens. You read articles, watch videos, or watch tournaments. You observe how the golfing greats drive, chip, and putt. You experiment with different balls, different clubs, different stances, and different grips. When you place your ball on the tee, you measure the distance, take your stance, get the proper grip. All of this is preparation. But when you actually swing the club, you do not think about the position of your right thumb, the elevation of your right heel, the curvature of your spine. You took care of those things before the swing.

Obviously, you are thinking about what you are doing when you swing the club, but you are not thinking of every detail of what you are doing. It is the same when we preach. We think about what we are doing, but not every detail.

Preaching, like every other discipline, requires hard work. You must invest yourself in your craft. Preaching is a lifetime discipline. The more you work at being effective, the more relaxed and the less preoccupied you will be when you preach. You must do your vocal exercises, do your practice preaching, and work on your oral interpretation before entering the pulpit. The result will be a blessing not only for you but also for your congregation.

## Question #9

I have heard some preachers say we should write our sermons in full and take our entire manuscript to the pulpit. I have heard other preachers say we should have only some brief notes with us when we preach. I have even known of some preachers who use no notes at all when they preach. Which of these methods do you recommend?

—

There is no pat answer to your question. I recommend that you use the method that works best for you. Let's see what the advantages and disadvantages are.

Very few preachers write their sermons word-for-word. This is especially true for preachers who prepare two or three sermons weekly. Those who do write sermon manuscripts say they can word their sermons more clearly, with more appeal, and with greater depth of thought. They say writing the manuscript allows them to pore over every word. They also say they don't have to think on their feet and risk saying something they would later regret. No doubt, what they say is true.

The main disadvantage of manuscript preaching that I have noticed is that the manuscript hinders delivery. Preachers who write manuscripts tend to read those manuscripts to the congregation. Eye contact, vocal variables, and body language usually suffer when the manuscript is read. Some manuscript preachers are notable exceptions. These exceptions are able to maintain 80–90 percent eye contact with no loss in effective delivery. But as a rule, the preachers who read manuscripts sacrifice effectiveness in sermon delivery.

Most preachers take some notes to the pulpit. The notes range anywhere from a few directional words to summary paragraphs. These preachers testify that their notes "keep them on track," especially if they are using body points. The notes remind them of the other details in the sermon—the proper time for an illustration, specifics of the illustration. Without their notes, these preachers say, they would lose their place and the sermon would meander and ramble.

Yet there are disadvantages of preaching with notes. Turning or shuffling pages may distract the congregation. The pulpit may lack space for both the Bible and notes. Rearranging the notes or finding your place in the notes may result in awkward pauses.

What can be said of the so-called extemporaneous preachers, those who use neither manuscript or notes? Of course, many of these are overly confident that their gift-of-gab will carry their sermon. These gift-of-gab preachers fool nobody, least of all their congregations. But some preachers are so thoroughly prepared that they can preach without notes. These deserve our attention.

These preachers have a mental capacity to organize a large amount of material. Even so, they are not entirely without notes. Most of them testify that key words in their biblical text are the cues for the movements or points or development of their sermons. These preachers also admit they find written notes awkward. As one such preacher said, "I am preaching just fine, then I think I should look at my notes. I stop preaching, I try to find my place. When I do, I reorganize my train of thought and resume preaching. But the long pause while I look at my notes has broken the flow of my sermon." This preacher almost inevitably forgets something important, only to remember it after the sermon.

You should use the system that works best for you. Too many individual differences exist for anyone to say that any one system is inherently better than any other system.

## Question #10

Is the study of sermon delivery relatively new? I don't remember hearing much about it when I first started preaching. Maybe our modern emphasis on the media has made us more conscious of delivery.

—

No doubt, the modern emphasis on the media has sharpened our awareness of sermon delivery. I think for a time we all wanted our delivery to be acceptable, but for the most part we were not too concerned about it. I used to hear preachers say, "Why study sermon delivery? After all, anybody can talk." The issue is not who can talk, but who can communicate. The content of our sermon travels at the speed of sound—about 700 miles per hour. The emotional part of our sermon (vocal variables, body language) travels at the speed of light—about 186,000 miles per second. (I know my analogy breaks down where the vocal variables are concerned, but hear me.) The congregation receives an impression from our delivery much more quickly than they do from our words. So, we really must give attention to our delivery. We must never forget, though, that the purpose of delivery is to *maximize the message and minimize the messenger.*

No, the emphasis on sermon delivery is not relatively new. I do think, however, we can discuss sermon delivery today in much more detail than was done in the past. We have access to much more information today than ever before. That is why, in conferences (and in books such as this one), we are trying to synthesize all the information and see how it relates to preaching. Hercules Collins in the seventeenth century and Spurgeon, Stalker, and Peter Cartwright in the nineteenth century all had something to say about sermon delivery.

Stalker delivered the Lyman Beecher Lectures on Preaching in 1891. I copied an excerpt from those lectures and am happy to share it with you.

The preacher ought to be master of the Oral Word. There is a stage which the truth has to pass through after it has been prepared in the study for the consumption of the hearers. This is the oral delivery; and it is a part of the natural history of the sermon which must not be overlooked. A sermon may be well composed in the study and yet be a failure in the pulpit. Indeed, this is one of the most critical stages of the entire process. There are few things more disappointing than to have received a message to deliver and spend a laborious and happy week in composition, and yet on Sunday, as you descend the pulpit stair, to know that you have missed the mark. This, however, is far from an infrequent occurrence. The same sermon may even be a success on one occasion, and on another a partial or a total failure.

Wherein a good delivery consists it is difficult to say. It is the rekindling of the fire of composition in the presence of the congregation; it is the power of thinking out the subject again on your feet. This must not be a mere repetition of a byegone process, but a new and original action of the mind on the spot. Tholuck, to whom I have already alluded in this lecture, says a sermon needs to be born twice: it must be born once in the study in the process of composition, and it must be born again in the pulpit in the process of delivery. Many a sermon is a genuine birth of the mind in the study which in the pulpit is still-born.

Some preachers have an extraordinary facility of putting themselves at once, and every time, in rapport with the audience, so that there is from first to last, whilst they speak, a commerce between the mind in the pulpit and the minds in the pews. To others this is the most difficult part of preaching. The difficulty is to get down amongst the people and to be actually dealing with them. Many a preacher has a thought, and is putting it into good enough words, but somehow the people are not listening and they cannot listen.

If the Senate of this University were ever to try the experiment of asking a layman to deliver this course of Lectures on Preaching, I am certain he would lay more stress on this than we do, and put a clear and effective—if possible, a graceful and eloquent—delivery among the chief desiderata of the pulpit. I do not know how it may be among you; but, when I was at college, we used rather to despise delivery. We were so confident in the power of ideas that we thought nothing of the manner of setting them forth. Only have good stuff, we thought, and it will preach itself. We like to repeat, with Faust,

"True sense and reason reach their aim
With little help from art and rule;
Be earnest! Then what need to seek
The words that best your meaning speak?"

So we thought; and many of us have since suffered for it. We know how many sermons are preached in the churches of the country every Sunday; but does anyone know how many are listened to? The newspapers supply us now and then with statistics of how many hearers are present in our congregations; but who will tell us what proportion of these are listeners? If we knew the exact percentage, I suspect, it would appall us. Yet it is not because there is not good matter in the sermons, but because it is not properly spoken. In the manufacture of steam-engines the problem is, I believe, to get as much work as possible out of the coal consumed. In every engine which has ever yet been constructed there has been a greater or less waste of heat, which is dispersed into the surrounding air or carried away by the adjacent portions of the machinery, without doing work. Engineering skill has been gradually reducing the amount of this waste and getting a larger and larger proportion of work out of the fuel; and a perfect engine would be one in which the whole of the coal consumed had its full equivalent in work done. One of our problems, it seems to me, is a similar one. There is an enormous disproportion between the amount of energy expended during the week in preparation and the amount of impression made on the hearers on Sunday. Ministers do not get enough of result in the attention, satisfaction and delight of their hearers for the work they do; and the failure is in the vehicle of communication between the study and the congregation—that is to say, in the delivery of the sermon. What I am pleading for is, that there should be more work to show for the coal consumed.[1]

▼

# APPENDIX A

## Self-Evaluation for Voice Quality

1. Were my vocal bands sore before, during, or after delivering the sermon?

2. Did I feel any vocal strain while preaching?

3. Do I hear any vocal strain in my preaching?

4. Was my optimum pitch level high during the sermon?

5. Was my breathing affected by tension before or during the sermon?

6. When I inhale, is it audible?

If any of the above questions are answered "yes," practice the exercises in chapter 1.

7. Using the form below, plot a graph for an entire sermon, indicating when your voice was clear and strong and when it may have become strained, perhaps causing a retreat to dramatic whisper.

    strong

    about
    right
    for me

    weak

Introduction    Body    Conclusion    Invitation

# APPENDIX B

## Self-Evaluation for Clear Speech

1. List any misarticulated sounds in your sermon:

2. Were these misarticulated sounds caused by lazy speech habits?

3. Did rapid speech cause you to slur some words?

If the answer to any of these questions is "yes," review chapter 2. Give special attention to the specific sounds you did not articulate clearly in your sermon.

## APPENDIX C

## Self-Evaluation for Vocal Variables

### Pitch

1. Were my inflections clear and sharp enough to communicate transitions?

2. Were my inflections clear and sharp enough to communicate emphases?

3. Was my use of pitch restricted to a narrow range?

4. Do I detect any monotonous patterns in pitch?

If any of these questions are answered "yes," turn to chapter 3 and review the information about pitch.

5. Using the form below, plot a graph of your entire sermon showing general variations in pitch. If pitch is being used effectively, it will be difficult to plot this graph. If pitch is patterned or in a narrow range, the graph will be relatively simple to plot.

(Form for question 5.)

_____ high
_____ pitch
_____
_____
_____
_____
_____ my
_____ optimum
_____ pitch
_____
_____
_____
_____
_____ weak
_____

Introduction     Body     Conclusion     Invitation

6. Plot a graph for a brief segment of your sermon, preferably where transitions and emphases occur. Beneath the graph, write

the sentence in which the transitions or emphases appear. Study the relationship between pitch and content. Does pitch support content?

(Form for question 6.)

_____ high
_____
_____
_____
_____
_____
_____
_____ optimum
_____
_____
_____
_____
_____
_____ low
_____

" _____ "

(Sentence)

**Volume**

1. Is volume loud most of the time?
2. Is volume soft most of the time?
3. Is there a predictable pattern in volume levels?
4. Am I loud during less significant segments of my sermon?
5. Am I soft during more significant segments of my sermon?

If the answer to any of these questions is "yes," review the information in chapter 4 about volume.

6. Plot a graph of the general volume level for your entire sermon. Again, this will be difficult if volume is used effectively, and relatively simple if volume is in a narrow range or a predictable pattern.

7. On the form provided on page 144, plot a graph for one of the key emphases of the sermon. If possible, write the words of this key segment beneath the graph and study the relationship between content and volume. Does volume support content?

8. Plot a similar graph for one of the less significant segments of the sermon. Check to see if volume was emphatic or if it was at a properly reduced level at this time.

_____
_____ high
_____
_____
_____
_____
_____
_____
_____
_____
_____
_____
_____ low
_____

Introduction      Body      Conclusion      Invitation

" _ _ _ _ _ _ _ _ _ _ _ _ _ _ _ _ _ _ _ _ _ _ _ _ _ _ _ _ _ _ _ _ _ _ _ "
(Key Words)

### Rate

1. Transcribe sixty seconds of your sermon from a tape. How many words did you transcribe? More than 150? Less than 100? If you count more than 150, determine if the content was relatively less significant, and that a rapid rate was justified. If you count less than 100, are you sure that content was that emphatic, and that your deliberate approach was justified?

2. Transcribe the entire sermon, using slashes (/) to isolate sixty-second segments. This will clearly outline where the rate was fast or slow, and if the rate varied much at all.

(Form for question 2.)

_____ 250 wpm
_____
_____ 200 wpm
_____
_____ 150 wpm
_____
_____ 100 wpm
_____
_____ 50 wpm
_____
_____

Introduction      Body      Conclusion      Invitation

### Pause

1. Use the transcription made for study of rate. With a different color ink, put a slash mark (\) between words that received a

pause. (Count only pauses of one second or more.) You may want to use different colors or varying sizes of slash marks to indicate longer or shorter pauses.

2. Review the transcript to see if any transitions or emphases did not receive a pause. (For instance, moving from the end of the reading of the text to the first word of the introduction.)

### Gestures and Facial Expressions

1. Did gestures and facial expressions coincide with content? (Did I smile when I spoke of Jesus?)

2. Did gestures and facial expressions say the same thing as content? (They should not precede or come after content has been spoken.)

3. Did gestures and facial expressions cause distractions? (Too many of them?)

4. Do I use a particular gesture or facial expression too often?

5. Are my gestures rhythmic?

6. Do my gestures and facial expression seem too dramatic?

Review the information and exercises in chapter 4 if questions 1 or 2 were answered "no" or if questions 3, 4, 5, or 6 were answered "yes."

## APPENDIX D

### Self-Evaluation of Oral Interpretation

1. Did delivery support content? Generally? Some of the time? Not often?

2. Was the Scripture read smoothly?

3. Did I communicate the ethos of the Scripture?

4. Did I communicate the ethos of the sermon?

5. Were the ethos of the Scripture reading and of the sermon at variance?

Review chapter 4 for information and exercises to help oral interpretation.

▼

# Bibliography

## Books

Abelman, Robert, and Stewart M. Hoover. *Religious Television: Controversies and Conclusions*. Norwood, N.J.: Ablex Publishing Corporation, 1990.

Barth, Karl. *The Preaching of the Gospel*. Translated by B. E. Hooke. Philadelphia: Westminster Press, 1963.

———. *The Word of God and the Word of Man*. Translated by Douglas Horton. London: Hodder and Stoughton, 1928.

Benson, Dennis. *Electric Evangelism*. Nashville: Abingdon Press, 1973.

Benthall, Jonathan, and Ted Polhemus, eds. *The Body as a Medium of Expression*. New York: E. P. Dutton and Co., 1975.

Broadus, John A. *A Treatise on the Preparation and Delivery of Sermons*. Revised by E. C. Dargan. New York: George H. Doran Co., 1898.

Brooks, Dieth, Eugene Bahn, and L. Lamont Okey. *The Communicative Act of Oral Interpretation*. Boston: Allyn and Bacon, Inc., 1975.

Brooks, Phillips. *Lectures on Preaching*. Grand Rapids: Baker Book House, 1978 reprint.

Brown, H. C., Jr., *A Quest for Reformation in Preaching*. Waco, Tex.: Word Books, 1968.

Brown, H. C., Jr., H. Gordon Clinard, Jesse J. Northcutt, and Al Fasol. *Steps to the Sermon*. Nashville: Broadman Press, 1963, rev. ed., 1996.

Caird, G. B. *The Language and Imagery of the Bible*. Philadelphia: Westminster Press, 1980.

Chartier, Myron R. *Preaching as Communication: An Interpersonal Perspective*. Abingdon Preacher's Library Series, ed. by William D. Thompson. Nashville: Abingdon Press, 1981.

Danielou, Jean. *Christ and Us*. Translated by Walter Roberts. New York: Sheed and Ward, 1961.

Eisenson, Jon. *Voice and Diction*. 3rd ed. New York: Macmillan, 1974.

Eisenson, Jon, and Paul H. Boase. *Basic Speech*. 3rd ed. New York: Macmillan, 1975.

Ellens, J. Harold. *Models of Religious Broadcasting*. Grand Rapids: Eerdmans, 1974.

Fore, William F. *Television and Religion: The Shaping of Faith, Values, and Culture*. Minneapolis: Augsburg, 1987.

Frankl, Razelle. *Televangelism: The Marketing of Popular Religion*. Carbondale, Ill.: Southern Illinois University Press, 1987.

Grasso, Domenico. *Proclaiming God's Message: A Study in the Theology of Preaching*. South Bend, Ind.: The University of Notre Dame Press, 1965.

Harper, Nancy. *Human Communication Theory: The History of a Paradigm*. Rochelle Park, N.J.: Hayden Books Co., Inc., 1979.

Hoover, Stewart M. *Mass Media Religion: The Social Sources of the Electronic Church: Communications and Human Values*. Newbury Park, Calif.: Sage Publications, Inc., 1988.

Hovland, Carl I., Irving L. Janis, and Harold H. Kelly. *Communication and Persuasion*. New Haven, Conn.: Yale University Press, 1953.

Hughey, Jim D., and Arlis W. Johnson. *Speech Communication: Foundations and Challenges*. New York: Macmillan, 1975.

Jackson, B. F., Jr. *You and Communication in the Church*. Waco, Tex.: Word Books, 1974.

Klepper, Joseph T. *The Effects of Mass Communication*. Glencoe, Ill.: Free Press, Inc., 1960.

Knapp, Mark L. *Nonverbal Communication in Human Interaction*. New York: Holt, Rinehart and Winston, 1972.

Lischer, Richard. *A Theology of Preaching: The Dynamics of the Gospel*. Abingdon Preacher's Library Series, ed. by William D. Thompson. Nashville: Abingdon Press, 1981.

Mehrabian, Albert. *Nonverbal Communication*. Chicago: Aldine-Atherton, 1972.

Oliver, Robert T. *History of Public Speaking in America*. Boston: Allyn and Bacon, Inc., 1965.

Olson, Alan M., Christopher Parr, and Debra Parr, eds. *Video Icons and Values*. Albany, N.Y.: State University of New York Press, 1991.

Ott, Heinrich. *Theology and Preaching*. Translated by Harold Knight. Philadelphia: Westminster Press, 1961.

Read, David H. C. *The Communication of the Gospel*. London: SCM Press, Ltd., 1952.

Rossiter, Charles M., Jr., and W. Barnett Pearce. *Communicating Personally: A Theory of Interpersonal Communication and Human Relationships*. New York: Bobbs-Merrill Co., 1975.

Sangster, W. E. *The Approach to Preaching*. Philadelphia: Westminster Press, 1952.

Sarrett, Lew, William Trufant Foster, and Alma Johnson Sarrett. *Basic Principles of Speech*. 3rd ed. Boston: Houghton Mifflin Co., 1958.

Schultze, Quentin J. *Redeeming Television: How TV Changes Christians—How Christians Can Change TV*. Downers Grove, Ill.: InterVarsity, 1992.

―――. *Televangelism and American Culture: The Business of Popular Religion*. Grand Rapids: Baker, 1991.

―――., ed. *American Evangelicals and the Mass Media: Perspectives on the Relationship between American Evangelicals and the Mass Media*. Grand Rapids: Zondervan (Academie Books), 1980.

Siegman, Aaron W., and Stanley Feldstein, eds. *Nonverbal Behavior and Communication*. New Jersey: Lawrence Erlbaum Associates, 1978.

Spurgeon, Charles Haddon. *Lectures to My Students*. Grand Rapids: Zondervan Press, 1945.

Steimle, Edmund A., Morris J. Niedenthal, and Charles L. Rice. *Preaching the Story*. Philadelphia: Fortress Press, 1980.

Stevenson, Dwight E., and Charles F. Diehl. *Reaching People from the Pulpit*. New York: Harper and Row, 1958.

Webber, Robert E. *God Still Speaks: A Biblical View of Christian Communication*. Nashville: Nelson, 1980.

## Articles

Bailey, Raymond. "Vital Preaching!" *Baptist Program* (November 1974).

Bluck, John. "Beyond Neutrality: A Christian Critique of the Media." *Risk Book Series*, no. 3 (1978).

Brooks, R. T., "Preaching in an Audio-Visual Age," *Baptist Quarterly* 29 (July 1981).

Dunnam, Spurgeon M., Jr. "Guidelines for the Church for Ministry Through the Mass Media." *Perkins Journal of Theology* 28 (Summer 1975).

Ellens, Harold J. "Psychodynamics in Mass Media Society" *Journal of Psychology and Theology* 7 (Fall 1979).

Fore, William F. "Communication: A Complex Task for the Church." *Christian Century,* 92 (July 1975).

Hesselgrave, David J. "'Gold From Egypt': The Contribution of Rhetoric to Cross-Cultural Communication." *Missiology,* 4 (January 1976).

Joregenson, Knud. "Models of Communication in the New Testament." *Missiology,* 4 (October 1976).

Kehl, D. G. "Have You Committed Verbicide Today?" *Christianity Today* 22 (January 1978).

Meister, J. W. Gregg. "Mass Media Ministry: Understanding Television." *Theology Today* 37 (October 1980).

Montgomery, John Warwick. "Mass Communication and Scriptural Proclamation." *The Evangelical Quarterly* 49 (January-March, 1977).

Muggeridge, Malcolm. "Christ and the Media." *Journal of the Evangelical Society* 21 (September 1978).

Nichols, J. Randall. "Towards a Theological View of Responsibility in Communication." *The Princeton Seminary Bulletin* 68 (Winter 1976).

Taylor, Roy. "So What?" *The Journal of Pastoral Practice* 4 no. 4 (1980).

Towne, Edgar A. "Communicating a Message and Believing a Message." *Encounter* 37 (Winter 1976).

Watson, Richard G. "What's Wrong with Preaching Today?" *Christianity Today* (October 25, 1975).

▼

# Notes

### Preface

1. H. C. Brown, Jr., *A Quest for Reformation in Preaching* (Waco, Tex.: Word Books, 1968), 5.

### Introduction

1. Domenico Grasso, *The Preaching of God's Message* (South Bend, Ind.: University of Notre Dame Press, 1965), 8.

2. Ibid., 20.

3. Cf. particularly *The Preaching of the Gospel,* trans. B. E. Hooke (Philadelphia: The Westminster Press, 1963); *The Word of God and the Word of Men,* trans. Douglas Horton, (1938); and *Church Dogmatics,* vol. 1, pt. 1, trans. G. T. Thomason (New York: Charles Scribner & Sons, 1936).

4. Barth, *The Preaching of the Gospel,* 21.

5. For example, see *Religion: Speeches to Its Cultural Despisers,*trans. John Omen (New York: Harper, 1958); George Cross, *The Theology of Schleiermacher* (Chicago: The University of Chicago Press, 1911); and Schleiermacher's *Liturgies: Theorie & Praxis* (Göttingen: Vandenhocck and Ruprecht, 1963).

6. Clyde Fant, *Preaching for Today* (New York: Harper and Row, 1975), 33.

### Chapter 1

1. Dwight E. Stevenson and Charles F. Diehl, *Reaching People from the Pulpit* (New York: Harper and Row, 1958), 40–41.

2. Jon Eisenson, *Voice and Diction,* 3rd ed. (New York: Macmillan, 1974), 38.

3. Billy Graham, "The Suffering Saviour on a Crimson Cross," in *Southern Baptist Preaching,* ed. H. C. Brown, Jr. (Nashville: Broadman Press, 1959), 68.

4. Lew Sarett, William Foster, and Alma Johnson Sarett, *Basic Principles of Speech,* 3rd ed. (Boston: Houghton Mifflin Co., 1958), 212.

5. Ibid., 225.

6. "G. Earl Guinn, "The Prophetic Ministry," in *Southern Baptist Preaching* (Nashville: Broadman Press, 1959), 95.

7. H. C. Brown, Jr., H. Gordon Clinard, and Jesse J. Northcutt, *Steps to the Sermon*, (Nashville: Broadman Press, 1963) 164.

## Chapter 2

1. Jon Eisenson's superb book *Voice and Diction*, 3rd ed. (New York: Macmillan, 1974) offers a detailed description and practical exercises for every sound in the English language.

## Chapter 3

1. For a brief review of the problem, see David Crystal's essay "Paralinguistics," in *The Body As a Medium of Expression*, ed. Jonathan Benthall and Ted Polhemus (New York: Dutton, 1975), 163–74.

2. An initial shock will occur at seeing the sermon in writing. Remember, oral and written styles differ. However, the transcript may reveal a need for further work in clarity of diction. For instance, one of my transcripts revealed an eighty-two word sentence! An important side benefit of the transcript is that it drives us to clearer thought patterns.

3. Don Sharp, "Will You Go? (Isaiah 6:1–8)," in *Southern Baptist Preaching Today: Dynamic Messages from Pastors Across America*, R. Earl Allen and Joel Gregory, comps. (Nashville: Broadman Press, 1987), 353–55.

4. Jess Moody, "The Most Encouraging Verse in the Bible," in *Southern Baptist Preaching Today*, 258–59.

5. Adrian P. Rogers, "Mending Broken Brothers (Galatians 6:1–2)," in *Southern Baptist Preaching Today*, 327.

6. Cristobal Doña, "The Discipline in the Church (Matthew 18:15–18)" in *Southern Baptist Preaching Today*, 67.

7. Perry R. Sanders, "A Portrait of Christ (John 5:1–9)," in *Southern Baptist Preaching Today*, 342–43.

8. Robert A. Baker, comp. and ed., H. C. Brown, Jr., "The Nature of Sin (Romans 6:23)" in *Southwestern Sermons* (Nashville: Broadman Press, 1960), 7–8.

9. *Walt Whitman's Poems*, ed. Gay Wilson Allen and Charles T. Davis (Washington Square, New York: New York University Press, 1955), 200.

10. G. Earl Guinn, "The Prophetic Ministry (Isaiah 6:1–13)," in *Southern Baptist Preaching*, 87.

11. Hershel Hobbs, "The Gospel of Isaiah (Isaiah 53)," in *Southern Baptist Preaching*, H. C. Brown, Jr., ed. (Nashville: Broadman Press, 1953), 98.

12. Robert G. Lee, "It Is Finished (John 19:30)," in *Southern Baptist Preaching*, 114.

13. Millard J. Berquist, "America's Number One Health Problem—Alcoholism," in *Southern Baptist Preaching*, 45, 55.

## Chapter 4

1. Sarrett, Foster, Sarrett, *Basic Principles*, 313.

2. Mark L. Knapp, *Nonverbal Communication in Human Interaction* (New York: Holt, Rinehart & Winston, 1972), 85–86.

3. Milton Ferguson, "What Is the Cross (Romans 5:6–8, RSV; Colossians 2:13–15; Mark 8:34)," in *Southern Baptist Preaching*, 83–84.

4. Joel C. Gregory, *Gregory's Sermon Synopses: 200 Expanded Summaries* (Nashville: Broadman Press, 1991), 165.

5. Don M. Kim, "The Gospel of Jesus Christ in Genesis 1–3," in *Southern Baptist Preaching Today*, 210–211.

6. Paul Powell, "How God Helps Us," in *Southern Baptist Preaching Today*, 292.

7. Calvin Miller, "The Evangelist as . . . the Rebel Lover," in *Southern Baptist Preaching Today*, 254–55.

8. Hercules Collins, *The Temple Repair'd* (London: William and Joseph Marshall, 1702), 29–30

**Chapter 5**

1. Keith Brooks, Eugene Bahn, LaMont Okey, *The Communicative Act of Oral Interpretation* (Boston: Allyn & Bacon, 1975), 25–26. Italics mine.

2. Ibid., 26.

3. Ibid., 155.

4. Sarrett, Foster, Sarrett, *Basic Principles*, 142.

**Chapter 6**

1. A. F. Harlow, *Old Wires and New Waves* (New York: Appleton-Century, 1936), 455.

2. John H. Court, "Paralinguistic Cues in Religious Broadcasting," *Journal of Psychological Theology* (Winter 1978): 40.

3. P. D. Holtzman, *The Psychology of Speakers' Audiences* (Glenview: Scott, Foresman, and Co., 1970), 7.

4. For an interesting account of the history of the fairness doctrine, see Fred Friendly, *The Good Guys and the Bad Guys: Free Speech vs. Fairness in Broadcasting* (New York: Random House, 1975).

5. For a brief discussion of preaching that is basic and vital see Raymond Bailey, "Vital Preaching," *Baptist Program* (November 1974): 4; and Richard G. Watson, "What's Wrong with Preaching Today?" *Christianity Today* (October 25, 1975): 27.

6. D. G. Kehl used this word in his incisive article, "Have You Committed Verbicide Today?" *Christianity Today* (January 28, 1978): 18–21.

7. John R. W. Stott, *Between Two Worlds: The Art of Preaching in the 20th Century* (Grand Rapids: Eerdmans, 1982), 70–73.

8. Ibid., 73.

9. Martin E. Marty, *The Improper Opinion* (Philadelphia: Westminster Press, 1961), 32.

10. Harold J. Ellens, *Models of Religious Broadcasting* (Grand Rapids: Eerdmans, 1974), 147.

11. Quentin J. Schultze, *Redeeming Television: How TV Changes Christians—How Christians Can Change TV* (Downers Grove, Ill.: InterVarsity, 1992), 13–14.

12. Paul S. Lazarsfeld and Robert K. Merton, "Mass Communication: Popular Taste, and Organized Social Action," in *The Process and Effects of Mass Communications*, eds. Wilburn Schramm and Donald E. Roberts (Chicago: University of Illinois Press, 1972), 561–62.

13. Fulton J. Sheen, *Life Is Worth Living* (Garden City, N.Y.: Garden City Books, 1953), viii.

**Chapter 7**

1. James Stalker, *The Preacher and His Models* (New York: George H. Doran Co., 1891), 117–21.

▼